WHY WE (STILL) NEED RUSSIAN LITERATURE

RUSSIAN SHORTS

Russian Shorts is a series of thought-provoking books published in a slim format. The Shorts books examine key concepts, personalities, and moments in Russian historical and cultural studies, encompassing its vast diversity from the origins of the Kievan state to Putin's Russia. Each book is intended for a broad range of readers, covers a side of Russian history and culture that has not been well-understood, and is meant to stimulate conversation.

Willard Sunderland, Henry R. Winkler Professor of Modern History, University of Cincinnati, USA

Published Titles

Pussy Riot: Speaking Punk to Power, Eliot Borenstein
Memory Politics and the Russian Civil War: Reds Versus Whites, Marlene Laruelle and Margarita Karnysheva
Russian Utopia: A Century of Revolutionary Possibilities, Mark Steinberg
Racism in Modern Russia, Eugene M. Avrutin
Meanwhile, In Russia: Russian Memes and Viral Video Culture, Eliot Borenstein
Ayn Rand and the Russian Intelligentsia, Derek Offord
The Multiethnic Soviet Union and Its Demise, Brigid O'Keeffe
Nuclear Russia, Paul Josephson
The History of Birobidzhan, Gennady Estraikh
The Afterlife of the 'Soviet Man': Rethinking Homo Sovieticus, Gulnaz Sharafutdinova
Jews under Tsars and Communists, Robert Weinberg
Russian Food since 1800: Empire at Table, Catriona Kelly

Upcoming Titles

Russia's History Painters: Vasily Surikov, Viktor Vasnetsov, and the Remaking of the Past, Stephen M. Norris
A Social History of the Russian Army, Roger R. Reese
A Territorial History of Russia, Paul Werth
Black Encounters with the Soviet Union, Maxim Matusevich
Gulag Fiction from Stalin to Putin, Polly Jones
The Invention of Russian Time, Andreas Scholne
The Tolstoy Marriage, Ani Kokobobo

WHY WE (STILL) NEED RUSSIAN LITERATURE

TOLSTOY, DOSTOEVSKY, CHEKHOV, AND OTHERS

Angela Brintlinger

BLOOMSBURY ACADEMIC

LONDON • NEW YORK • OXFORD • NEW DELHI • SYDNEY

BLOOMSBURY ACADEMIC
Bloomsbury Publishing Plc
50 Bedford Square, London, WC1B 3DP, UK
1385 Broadway, New York, NY 10018, USA
29 Earlsfort Terrace, Dublin 2, Ireland

BLOOMSBURY, BLOOMSBURY ACADEMIC and the Diana logo are trademarks of
Bloomsbury Publishing Plc

First published in Great Britain 2024
Copyright © Angela Brintlinger, 2024

Series design by Tjaša Krivec

Photograph: Tetra Images © Getty Images

A catalogue record for this book is available from the British Library.

A catalog record for this book is available from the Library of Congress.

ISBN: HB: 978-1-3502-4215-9
PB: 978-1-3502-4214-2
ePDF: 978-1-3502-4216-6
eBook: 978-1-3502-4217-3

Typeset by Newgen KnowledgeWorks Pvt. Ltd., Chennai, India
Printed and bound in Great Britain

To find out more about our authors and books visit www.bloomsbury.com
and sign up for our newsletters.

CONTENTS

ACKNOWLEDGMENTS

I've been working on this book for over a decade, I would say, and thus have racked up many debts along the way. Its roots are in my personal blog, *The Manic Bookstore Café*, which I have used as a space to muse on culture, art, literature, teaching, reading, students, and travel. When I started that project in 2012, the idea of writing on the internet was still somewhat new, but because I was living abroad (initially in China for a few weeks and then in Poland for a semester), I used the blog to feel a connection to family back home and to share my experiences with my mother, Ginny, and my sister, Rose. Both commented on things I wrote and made me think it was worth trying to develop that voice.

I would never have started blogging if not for my daughter Olivia, who at twelve at the time was too young to have her own online presence. Pretty quickly it became clear that a blog was not something that one shared, and she left me to manage the *Manic Bookstore Café* on my own. About that same time, I created a blog for Yellow Springs High School AP English students, whom I challenged to read *Anna Karenina* over the winter holidays. As I wrote, I imagined them moving through the book with me and gave context and pointers to help them understand what they were reading. Of course, it turns out that the blog address had never been communicated to them so I was writing into the void … but isn't that what writing often turns out to be? The important thing is not so much to have an audience as to imagine one. A few years later I did have a high-school audience, some young people for whom I created a "Russian studies workshop," and we read together throughout one academic year, meeting biweekly at the ever hospitable Antioch College Library—in fact, in a classroom where Rod Serling used to teach. I want to thank Scott Sanders for helping us find a home there.

As I began to think about honing my online voice for print publication, I was aided by my friends and fellow scholars Catherine O'Neil and Megan Dixon. They patiently talked me through various iterations of the manuscript and offered useful opinions and thoughtful suggestions. I was encouraged to complete a draft by Steve Norris, who has been unfailingly enthusiastic about the project as we moved slowly toward publication. Steve1, as I call him, and his Miami University buddies formed a short story reading group during the pandemic and welcomed me into it with open arms. As the only literary scholar in a room, even a virtual one, of historians, I had to justify my arguments in new ways, and I'm honored that Matthew Gordon, Erik Jenson, and Steve Conn took me seriously. When Steve1 invited me to submit the book to Russian Shorts, I was thrilled. I am grateful to the anonymous referees for the proposal and most especially to Caryl Emerson whose sage advice has improved the final product immensely. Students from the distant and not so distant past have joined me on this journey, and I have loved sharing their voices and their smart reactions to Russian literature with readers.

More than anyone I need to thank Steve2, my husband and partner, without whom nothing would ever move forward. He makes me laugh, and he keeps me centered.

CHAPTER 1
INTRODUCTION: WHY WE NEED RUSSIAN LITERATURE

Madmen and Lovers. I used to hang out at a coffee shop with this name, and it attracted the usual suspects—people with long hair, some in hippy clothing, moms (or sometimes dads) and their babies. The café featured comfy couches and armchairs, the walls were lined with bookcases, and every table had a couple of old hardbacks or tattered paperbacks on it. Though I often brought my own book, or a writing project, I inevitably thumbed through whatever was lying around. Books are like that. They lure you in, as much by their covers, typeface, and paper—thick and luscious or tissue-thin—as by their contents. *Madmen and Lovers* didn't have a Russian theme, but it might as well have. Ivan Turgenev, Anna Akhmatova, Lyudmila Petrushevskaya, Joseph Brodsky, and of course Anton Chekhov: there were always Russian authors represented at the café and plenty of patrons glancing through their pages. There are cafés like this all over the world—I've visited similar ones in Budapest and Xi'an, in Warsaw and London and Genoa, in Boston and Austin. And I've found the Russians everywhere I go.

As a professor of Russian literature at a large American university in the Midwest, I have spent almost three decades teaching Russian books. I've had a lot of students—and a lot of different types of readers—pass through my classrooms. But one thing I always brag about: if you sign up for my class, you've read a novel, and you want to read another one. Students of Russian literature are among the most interesting, engaged, and enthusiastic. Even when they discover they have leapt into the deep end without a life jacket.

I am as sympathetic to readers who are intimidated by works of literature steeped in historical detail and filled with unfamiliar names as I am to student complaints that sometimes Russian novels require too much attention, especially in a semester filled with physics labs and psychology tests. Russia, though, intrigues readers and draws them in, even when, or perhaps because, historical or current events highlight the country's status as an enigmatic place where patterns of decision-making on the level of central government and in the lives of ordinary people don't seem to map onto our own. In this volume I argue that we need Russian literature. The books I have loved and taught, and that my students have struggled or raced through, bring lasting rewards.

Literature with a capital L can sometimes be found in airport bookshops and at bookstore cafés. It can always be found in libraries and at universities. And it encompasses books of all kinds: long ones and short ones, boring ones and complicated ones. Literature differs from just reading material (what in Russian is called *chtivo*) because it demands—and rewards—close attention, repeated readings and rereadings, extended mulling over. In these pages we will explore why.

People—faculty, journalists, social commentators—sometimes despair over the decline of the humanities and over a perceived lack of interest in investing precious college hours and dollars in reading and discussing long or complicated texts. Students (and their parents, more to the point) want to acquire marketable skills, want their major to be the name of a future profession. And it's true. Being an accountant pays well enough and is a stable job. But taking exclusively accounting classes in college does not offer the best preparation for post-college life. Literature is there to help.

For nearly two centuries, readers all over the world have found the great canon of Russian literature to be inspiring and heartbreaking, exotic and familiar. Love and death, war and peace, crime and punishment (and madness too); readers across the globe have found in Russian writing a substantial measure of intellectual provocation, aesthetic pleasure, emotional resonance, and personal solace. *Why We (Still) Need Russian Literature* makes the case that literature plays an important role in our emotional and intellectual lives, and Russian literature in particular fulfills many of the needs of readers who want to think deeply about life, death, and the role an individual can play in our larger society.

To make this argument across this short book, I use a number of authors from Russia to connect readers with these experiences, and in so doing I argue that texts like these can and should be revisited over the course of our lives. What seemed boring or off-putting at twenty might prove fascinating or insightful to a reader at forty. The literature that bears reading and rereading, contemplating and discussing, is the kind of literature we have always needed. This is the kind of literature we need now.

Looking at the specific ways in which writers from Russia have engaged the human condition, I use close readings to explain why these writers continue to be on the "must read" shelf of your neighborhood bookstore and public library, or why they should be if they are not. Each chapter focuses on one author and (his) works in one or more genres. I usually have to define the word genre for my students, so I'll do so now as well: I don't mean *genre fiction*, but rather mostly novels and short stories, with a play, some letters, a couple of related films thrown in. When teaching, I also usually define prose—writing in sentences rather than lines, in paragraphs rather than stanzas—but then I start my students off with a novel in (rhymed) verse just to make sure they experience the full spectrum of Russian literature.

In the following four chapters, I take the reader through a variation of my introduction to Russian literature course. But before we get there, I want to pause to think about books more generally and about the specific problems, and perks, of reading the Russians. We can start with the giant himself, Leo Tolstoy (1828–1910).

The Writer's (Bedside) Table

In an October 25, 1891 letter responding to a newspaperman's query, Tolstoy wrote out a list of what he considered his "most influential" books, a list that could be seen as a variant of "Tolstoy's bedside table."

This idea, of books towering at the side of a great writer's bed, is immensely evocative. I've seen the image used by other writers as well. It is effective, I think, for a number of reasons. First, as we imagine ourselves in the intimate space of a famous person, we feel like we are "in the know," getting the lowdown, somehow special to have this insight and access. Second, the very idea of a bedside table implies creative chaos—a table is not a shelf, and the books will be haphazardly stacked, perhaps in no particular order, perhaps with some spilling onto the floor nearby, and will require that we interpret them, intuit their significance, bring our own creativity to bear. Finally, though we admire famous writers, we also envy their talent, and by imagining this stack of books we reassure ourselves (or indeed are reassured by the writers themselves, if they are describing the state of a bedside table to outsiders) that all that brilliance does not emerge from thin air. Just as we read the master, the master has read someone else, indeed many someone elses.

The bedside table is not the only possible image. For example, when Philip Roth donated his personal library to the Newark Public Library, he gave readers access to it as laboratory. His books are heavily annotated and he imagined them shelved in thematic groupings: research and background reading for each novel placed together. Being able to see the bibliography and notes like this brings us into the author's creative process. With autobiographies, memoirs, maybe nowadays radio interviews, biopics, and blogposts, the experience of stepping into the lab has become more common, but for authors from other eras it can be a rare treat.

Tolstoy's list—like everything Tolstoy did, or so it seems—is idiosyncratic and a little obsessive compulsive (and not, therefore, the sprawling stack of books I conjured earlier). He adds parameters to the category of "influential books": first, he divides the lists into periods, the years in his life when he was influenced by them; and second, he gives them grades, starting with "enormously influential." The fact that some books will leave a stronger impression on a reader than others seems obvious. But learning in what ways individual writers, the ones we are reading, parse those differences and imagining how that informs what we know of their creative output brings them home to us. When we think about our own lives—our reading lives, if not our writing lives—we might imagine a similar sifting and winnowing. And if our reading habits are analogous in some ways to the reading habits of a great writer, we suddenly become kin to the author.

Tolstoy's list also takes me back to another time, when book publishing was a very different endeavor. Now we think of books, and movies, as being "age-appropriate," and publishers even categorize them that way. (The rise of YA, or "young adult," fiction is indicative of marketing techniques, but also tells us something about how modern publishers, librarians, and even parents try to guarantee a book's success among readers. Barbara Feinberg, in her 2004 book *Welcome to Lizard Motel*, advances the argument that YA "problem novels" can actually damage American children.) But in the contemporary world books are often written that way—some authors are children's book authors, while others target the adolescent or the adult. When Mark Haddon published his 2003 *Curious Incident of the Dog in the Night-Time* in both children's and adult categories, he did so in an effort to reach a broad audience and figuring—correctly, it seems to me—that the publisher's categories would drive away his potential grown-up readers.

But it wasn't always like that, and when Tolstoy identifies which books meant what to him at which period of his life, he gives us another path to understanding him and his writing. This list is convenient, an "in" for us to contemplate writer-as-reader. Of course, it's not the only way to get to know a writer. In many cases we can find out what authors read from their diaries, their memoirs, their correspondence. We can also just dive into their works and make our own judgments as to who or what might have influenced them. You don't need to read Pushkin to read Tolstoy, but Tolstoy had to read him in order to become Tolstoy. Those connections, once we know them, enrich our experience.

Literature in Translation: A Particular Challenge, a Particular Pleasure

As a lover of foreign languages and cultures, I do read in the original language when I can. When I can't, I love to read in translation, and

I am not alone. People turn to literature in translation as a way to travel, to try in the comfort of their own homes to experience the sights, sounds, and smells of another place entirely. We can do that with realist fiction especially because novels and short stories are filled with geographical features, climatological data, clothing choices, modes of transportation: the stuff of everyday life. Caryl Emerson describes the Russian "19th century mega-novelists" as taking readers with them on a "route to realism," with particularities, vivid landscapes, nuanced insights into characters and societies. But letters, memoirs, and travel writing are also full of detail. The sticky parts of language—names, jokes, sayings, customs—remind us that this is someone else's world and time, not ours. But in contrast to the more intimate forms of literature like the letter or diary, the novel gives us a breadth of perspective and a vast cast of characters with whom we can utterly lose ourselves. As Saul Morson has said, "Length is far from an accidental feature in novels."

This wide expanse can turn some readers off, and with Russian literature, the cast of characters can be a stumbling block. Russian names are notorious. They are difficult both because they are foreign and because they have many variants. I start my introductory Russian literature course off with a whole explanation of names: how the patronymic works, why the spellings and forms can differ, and how names sometime convey pronunciation norms or can even transmit additional information about social class or degree of intimacy. It can be nice to get those cultural explanations, and my students profit from them, but it's part of the journey, really, to have no idea how to pronounce names. When I read novels set in Nigeria I find myself identifying "the boyfriend character whose name starts with O" and not even reading to the end of the name. That's what my students do with the R character in *Crime and Punishment* (which causes a real problem, since there are two, Raskolnikov and Razumikhin). Do we need to know the background—the history, the culture, the original language—in order to understand the literature? In my classroom I am available as a cultural guide, but in fact readers can usually figure things out on their own, and that process can also be part of the pleasure.

Reading literature in translation is different from reading in the original language. Sometimes it may feel like you are not experiencing what the author had in mind, or that some nuance is missing. This is one of the reasons that famous novels get retranslated over and over— new generations want to get it right. For example, Tolstoy's novel of love and deceit, *Anna Karenina*, was first translated into English in 1886. In 2004 it was all the rage in the United States in the new translation by Larissa Volokhonsky and Richard Pevear. That year Oprah Winfrey featured it on her widely broadcast television talk show, and the husband-and-wife translation team have since gone on to rework most of modern Russian literature. Volokhonsky is a native speaker of Russian, and Pevear is not, so she gives a rough translation, he "Englishizes" it, and they go back and forth until they are satisfied. The results are sometimes spot on and sometimes quite far from the Tolstoyan (or Chekhovian, or Gogolian, etc.) original. It may be that every translation sparks a new translation from a new lover of literature and language who thinks she or he can get it right.

But plenty of people read whatever old copy they find lying around. When the translation gets in the way, it can be instructive to read through it, to push against it, to try to figure out why something sounds awkward. Reading older translations also gives us the chance to think about the special access they grant us to their own time. It can also be annoying, which is another reason new translations of *Anna Karenina*—and of other Russian novels—continue to appear.

About those names. Even here we run into translation problems. Vladimir Nabokov (1899–1977), who was a pedant and literalist if there ever was one, believed that Tolstoy's novel should be called *Anna Karenin* in English. He believed that for English-language speakers it makes no sense that Anna's surname is not the same as her husband's. Why the extra vowel?

That's something that is worth explaining, and if Nabokov had been more patient, he might have developed a whole cultural lesson for his Cornell students around this very question. Just as a vowel at the end of a first name often refers to gender (Anna, but also Natalia, Tatiana, Vera, and Ekaterina), so too in Russian you can usually tell someone's gender from their surname. Anna Karenina has a nice rhythm and an almost rhyming quality to it. Tolstoy chose the name for a reason. Perhaps because it mimics a "double dactyl"—a term we use in poetry to refer to two sets of three syllabus with the first syllable of each set stressed. (In Anna's case, the word boundary is in the wrong place, but the second syllable stress in KarENina makes her name a dactylic line nonetheless.)

My own name is a double dactyl, though my parents may not have been aware of it. What they did know, and what Tolstoy knew, is there is an aesthetic pleasure to be had in the sound of a double dactyl, one that Nabokov as a poet should have appreciated. And he may have, in Russian. In English he had different aesthetic and pedantic goals. On the question of Anna's name, I wholeheartedly disagree with him.

When translators leave the final "a" on Anna's surname, they remind us that we are reading in translation. The husband and wife have different surnames: why? Anna is living her life in a place, time, and language foreign to many English-language readers, even though sometimes that language is French, German, Italian, or even her own version of English. Keeping this reminder in the forefront helps us notice those details which we don't understand and think about what they might tell us.

It also forces us to let some things go. When we're reading a literary work, we have to be willing to sometimes not understand everything, and to have that be part of the pleasure. Do we really need to comprehend all the political intrigues of government in St. Petersburg, or can we be content to know that Karenin is an important official, and Anna is so estranged from him psychologically, emotionally, and intellectually, that she has no idea what he does for a living? That situation is not limited to the Russian empire in the second half of the nineteenth century. It happens today. It can happen to you.

So, while reading in the original is often an aspiration for book lovers, there's no real need to master the original language before tackling literary works. I like to encourage my students—many of whom are reading different translations of any work I assign—to think about what "translation" really means, not only from one language to another, but also from one culture (Russian, aristocratic) to another

(American, or British, or Caribbean), from one time period to another (eighteenth or nineteenth century to the twentieth—when I started teaching—and to the twenty-first century now). The past, after all, is also a foreign country, as writer L. P. Hartley so perceptively noted. When we read, we are partaking of the foreign and making it our own. That is what reading a novel from another tradition gives us: adventure and misadventure, comprehension and confusion, the feeling of peeking into someone else's life and perhaps of finding one's own truth there as well.

The Ideal Reader

We've looked now at what it means to read a literary text from a foreign place and at some of the specific problems with *Russian* literature. What remains is to briefly discuss what this book is not, and who is not included in it.

While I draw on some of my colleagues—other scholars, translators, teachers—and I explore their ideas, this is not a scholarly book. I prefer not to quote or cite from other critics in these chapters or to place the ideas into a larger scholarly conversation. There are plenty of studies and monographs that do that kind of work. What I do here instead is to move through concepts, authors, and texts to talk about how and why I think books like these matter and what we experience when we let ourselves enter their worlds. I draw on some of the writers I love whose insights I have cherished and I hope they speak to my readers as well.

Much of this will be retrospective. Although fresh books can be exhilarating, and despite the pull of the words "smashing debut novel" on the cover of a newly published work of fiction, I still want to read and reread the ones that have legs. In 1928 Yuri Tynianov—a creative and interesting Russian novelist only now beginning to get really good English translations—wrote: "it is difficult for a contemporary to see the magnitude of contemporary times and even harder to see a new word in it." In that same essay Tynianov commented that contemporaries, even great ones, couldn't see greatness in their own days: Dostoevsky was certain that Tolstoy had not "said a new word" in his fiction, even though by the time he made that statement Tolstoy had already written *War and Peace*, a novel read and reread across the world to this day. It's so hard to tell what will last, what will speak to people. "The question of greatness is decided by the centuries," Tynianov went on to assert; it's easier to look back than to perceive our own times. This from a historical novelist. He practiced what he preached.

When people ask me about my profession, I sometimes reply "I am a literature professor. I get a paycheck for reading books, for thinking, talking, and writing about them." Sounds idyllic, doesn't it? As a classroom instructor who gets to write her own syllabi, I am the expert; I am the one who chooses which books my students should read and who decides what knowledge I think they should be gaining from their reading and our discussions. I influence those students, and I benefit from their readings as well. Throughout this book I will draw on student insights and experiences, although it is not a memoir or a book about pedagogy or about how to teach literature in the classroom.

The beauty of teaching Russian literature at a large public university is that students in my classes have ranged in age from seventeen to seventy (though not too many of the latter). They may have read *Crime and Punishment* before coming to college; they may love the poetry of Bob Dylan or Dylan Thomas or they may have not read any poetry since high school (or even there). Frequently they have no idea of history, chronology, narrative, genre. (Who came first, they sometimes ask, the Victorians or Shakespeare?) Working with them has enabled me to value the literature I love, and the country and language I've been engaged with all my life, without necessarily insisting that they follow my path. It also forces me not to be lazy or make assumptions, which enriches my own readings of this and other literature as well.

For example, one student stayed after class to explain how *Master and Margarita* reminded him of some beloved fantasy authors, and he named some books and movies he was sure I would like. Another, hearing my argument that through fiction we can travel to new places, thought I should read his favorite travel essayist. Recently I found an old email from a student who was scarred by a bad experience in drama class with a Chekhov play but who was certain from my lecture that Chekhov must be great. What stories did I particularly like and why? I sent him a list. A colleague in the math department recently admitted to me that he was a long-haired undergraduate in my lit course when I was a brand new assistant professor—and he was reminded of how I introduced him to Russian literature by one of his own students, with whom he loved to talk about Dostoevsky. Turns out that young man had taken my course as well.

Literature courses at the college level sometimes get pretty far into the weeds of critical theory, so far that they leave the literature on the wayside. I love what Rita Felski has written: "Any attempt to clarify the value of literature must surely engage the diverse motives of readers and ponder the mysterious event of reading, yet contemporary theories give us poor guidance on such questions. We are sorely in need of richer and deeper accounts of how selves interact with texts." She is part of why I want to share my own observations about the act of reading, about what has moved my students to read and what texts speak to them in new ways. That notion of how the self interacts with the text is one of the subjects of my book.

Indeed, the ideal reader may be the serial rereader. I'd like to convince my readers to take that challenge. Nabokov, in his discussions of who the reader is, talked about a "good reader," a "gifted," "excellent," "admirable" reader. In his opinion, it is for that reader alone that the author writes:

The admirable reader does not seek information about Russia in a Russian novel, for he knows that the Russia of Tolstoy or Chekhov is not the average Russia of history but a specific world imagined and created by an individual genius. The admirable reader is not concerned with general ideas: he is interested in the particular vision. He likes the novel not because it helps him to get along with the group … he likes the novel because he imbibes and understands every detail of the text, enjoys what the author meant to be enjoyed, beams inwardly and all over, is thrilled by the magic imageries of the master-forger, the fancy-forger, the conjuror, the artist. Indeed, of all the characters that a great artist creates, his readers are the best.

This insight—that readers are actually created by authors—is one we might expect from Nabokov, who lands on some of the "banned book" lists that circulate in communities and requires a trigger warning when I teach him in class. He is if anything always opinionated. He is also frequently right—especially in the way he takes us inside characters' minds and into the creative process itself.

The actress Emily Mortimer, who portrayed a bookshop owner in a 2018 film, recently wrote about reading Nabokov as an adult. *Lolita*, she argues, is worth reading today (even in our #MeToo era) because (1) it's very funny; (2) it's written in beautiful prose; (3) it's filled with emotional honesty; (4) it's a beautiful love story. Beyond this, it provokes the reader's empathy—empathy for a monster, a criminal, a hateful and manipulative white European male—which is, she says, "the greatest measure of our humanity." Experiencing that empathy is a central part of enjoying literary works, and especially of talking about them with others. Nabokov, himself a dead white man of European extraction, can evoke love and hatred, sometimes simultaneously. And that's okay.

In my teaching I have used *Lolita*, an English-language American novel, as a window into nineteenth-century Russian literature. For students who find *Lolita* to be triggering I offer an alternative: the mildest and sweetest of Nabokov's novels, the lovely *Pnin*. I'm also keen on *Luzhin's Defense*, a novel that juxtaposes Russian life in Russia and émigré Europe, and I teach Nabokov's poetry as well, particularly his stanzas about translating Pushkin's novel-in-verse *Eugene Onegin*. His uncharacteristically self-deprecating description of that effort—leaving "dove droppings on your monument"—signals how difficult translation can be, not just for the reader but for the translator him or herself.

Though in my introductory course I steer away from criticism, I always share Nabokov's essay about good readers with my students.

To know that the author respects us, the readers, is to know that we have power too. We—readers all over the world of national as well as translated fiction—decide what literary works are worth reading. And we return to them over and over. Let's dig in and talk about *why*.

CHAPTER 2
IN THE BEGINNING THERE WAS PUSHKIN

Recently the countries that emerged three decades ago from the USSR have been scrubbing Russian influences from their cities and towns in response to Russia's invasion of Ukraine. Ukrainians and Latvians and many others have been asking themselves: why did we so love Russian literature? Or more precisely, why did we give in to imperial educational policies and accept these statues and place names as our own? The reputation of poet Alexander Pushkin has suffered as a result, as Moldovans and Georgians have asked: Why did we agree to admire Pushkin to such an extent that our landscapes became Russified? The tropes of Russian culture that were embraced by people across the Russian, Soviet and post-Soviet empires—statements like "Pushkin is our all" (Apollon Grigoriev) or "Pushkin is the sun of our poetry" (Vladimir Odoevsky)—are now being revealed as a form of Russian imperialism.

In this chapter I aim to talk about why *Russians* so love Pushkin and why he represents something valuable for non-Russians as well. I recently had a conversation with a Korean-American guy who runs a kiosk at Dulles Airport. The Russians, he insisted, wrote significantly more lasting works than American writers he had read. As I waited for my international flight, we had the chance to talk about Dostoevsky, Tolstoy, and Pushkin.

Such encounters always reassure me that it's possible to love Russian literature even when some aspects of the works are very specific. It's certainly true that Russian texts can seem to speak mostly to each other and do not always "translate" for an international audience. Names, dates, relationships, the class system including nobility, peasantry, and other categories, the integral role of the military, the continued importance of the Russian Orthodox religion: all these particulars can get in the way for a more general reader. But a little primer on names, a quick chronology and a brief introduction or a few historical footnotes can ease that reader's path into a Russian world that participates in and resonates with a more global experience.

My favorite Russian works take me on a journey with them, to new, exotic lands or to more familiar locales, into emotional landscapes that I know well or to dark places I hope never to experience myself. Those journeys make Russian literature attractive to all kinds of travelers. I sometimes wonder whether it is the vast expanses of the Russian empire itself (and of both the Soviet empire and the Russian Federation) that make travel such an innate part of Russian literature, or whether logistical restrictions—due to everything from government policies to financial considerations to extreme weather conditions—are what make the road a central trope in Russian letters. The borders of the imperial state have expanded or contracted, but it has always been huge.

One of the most intriguing Russian writers is Alexander Pushkin (1799–1837). He was an author of Russian firsts: the first professional writer, the first who hoped to live by his pen, the first who found an audience among French, German, and English readers, the first who tried his hand at virtually every genre and wrote virtuosic work in all of them. His novel-in-verse, *Eugene Onegin*, is one of those tours-de-force.

The world knows *Onegin* best in its operatic version by Tchaikovsky, and most casual listeners of classical music would recognize the sweeping *Polonaise* that frequently gets airtime on the radio. For that reason, some music critics go so far to suggest that Pushkin was not only the "father of Russian literature," but also the father of Russian opera. Composers from Glinka to Stravinsky have drawn on his plots—including *Onegin*—for their work. Pushkin's *Eugene Onegin* is a masterpiece that set the tone for much of what followed in his own literary career and more broadly throughout nineteenth-century Russia. The book was written over the course of almost eight years (1824–31) and features an intricate poetic form to render what can feel like fairly banal content.

The simple plot makes *Onegin* a successful opera: unrequited love, a dramatic duel, an unexpected comeuppance for the once jaded hero. Marital fidelity in the face of real temptation. But it's not the plot that keeps us reading Pushkin's novel. Chapters consist of stanzas and rhymed, metered lines, and the aesthetic experience of the form is at least as important as the conversations the novel engenders, even though those conversations can be important: about society and serfdom, about education and honor, about gender roles and the fate of individuals in a changing society.

Onegin is a great introduction to Russian literature, and to Russia, and I love to start my "masterpieces of Russian literature" course with it. For me, that's the beginning of our journey. It's a novel that demonstrates just how deeply this classic Russian author was steeped in European traditions, how much those things that later generations find to be quintessentially Russian actually emerged from European ways of thinking and even European literary types. Indeed, Russian literature of the nineteenth century was highly influenced by literary trends on the continent, in Great Britain, even in the United States. For example, Pushkin's contemporaries loved James Fennimore Cooper and read him in real time, though most didn't know English. French translations of Cooper's work were available to them almost as soon as he published a new novel in English. For Pushkin, literature had to suffice. Despite his dreams of travel to foreign lands, he never crossed the borders of the Russian empire. He had to let his reading do the traveling for him.

As a result, when you read Pushkin, Russia doesn't seem quite that foreign after all. In my course, we consider those European roots, and we also focus on how the playfulness and erudition we find in the novel help set a bar for what a "masterpiece" really is—in Russia and beyond.

A Devil of a Difference

In a letter to his friend Pyotr Vyazemsky in November 1823, Alexander Pushkin described the work he had recently embarked upon in these words: "I am writing not a novel, but a novel in verse: a devil of a difference!" Vyazemsky himself was a lover of travel, and in his own writing he chronicled life on the road, not always in flattering terms. (Anyone who has stayed in a roadside motel in the United States or a hotel near a European train station can probably relate to Vyazemsky's, and Pushkin's, complaints about inadequate inns and accommodations.) The correspondence between these two literary men reminds us how Russian literature was configured. The topic of the road was one the poets discussed in their letters and in their literary works, where they referred to each other in encoded conversations that were playful and as deliberately allusive as they could be elusive for readers. For the writers this was part of the game.

Pushkin earned his early fame primarily by publishing narrative poems, although he also wrote a host of lyrical verse, odes, and other poetry. His *Ruslan and Ludmila* (1820) took fairy tale motifs from Iranian, Finnish, and other traditions to offer a Romantic story of hapless giants, evil wizards, and fair maidens. Some of his youthful efforts had gotten him banned from St. Petersburg, then capital of tsarist Russia, and while ostensibly engaged in government service in the empire's southern climes Pushkin fell under the spell of George Byron and spun long poems on exotic themes. But then he realized: "I'm not Byron, I'm someone else."

This line comes from a poem penned by Mikhail Lermontov in 1832, but it could easily have sprung from Pushkin's lips as he strove to differentiate himself almost a decade earlier from the English bard. Lermontov wrote:

Нет, я не Байрон, я другой,	No, I'm not Byron, I'm another,
Еще неведомый избранник,	As yet an unknown chosen one,
Как он, гонимый миром странник,	Like him, a traveler persecuted by the world,
Но только с русскою душой.	But with a Russian soul.

The Russian soul is something Russians themselves love to exoticize, and foreign readers try to pin it down: just how *is* it different from any other soul? Is there something *national* about Russian suffering, persecution, self-focus? Or is it really just a hangover from Byron? These questions are quite relevant to Pushkin's novel-in-verse.

Though he claimed to Vyazemsky in that letter that the new book would be "sort of like *Don Juan*," Byron's famous satirical epic poem, Pushkin was aware that his decision to continue to write in verse, but to leave the traditional narrative poem behind and create something wholly new, was a momentous one. The qualities he brought together in this work—something familiar, but something his own, a classic storyline, but pushing up against boundaries in the artistic culture of tsarist Russia and of a broader Europe—help make *Eugene Onegin* the masterpiece it is.

For us, modern readers, who can plow through the entire novel in one sitting if we want, the experience of reading *Eugene Onegin* could not be more different from that of Pushkin's contemporaries. Having begun the novel on May 9, 1823 ("old style," i.e., according to the Julian calendar), Pushkin spent half a year writing the first two chapters and finally published chapter one in 1825. As that year drew to a tumultuous close with the unexpected death of Tsar Alexander I and the subsequent Decembrist revolt, the Russian political climate changed radically, and Pushkin had to respond. He certainly slowed down his writing, put the brakes on his publication schedule and may have shifted gears from his original intentions for the novel.

In the end—as Pushkin carefully documented—he spent "7 years, 4 months, and 17 days" composing his masterwork. He printed the chapters one at a time, revised and threw out some variant lines, stanzas and even chapters, and finally published the full eight-chapter work in one volume in 1833. This type of serial publication was common in the nineteenth century, and we know about it from Dickens and Dostoevsky, but the publication of *Eugene Onegin* was more protracted than most. For Pushkin and this novel, the manner of composition and the delayed pace of publication had real significance for how the work developed.

Why should today's reader care about the composition of this novel, and how might it change the way we read the book? Well, for one thing, I don't recommend charging through *Eugene Onegin* in one session. The novel was composed slowly, and over those many years both Pushkin and the country he lived in experienced significant changes. Pushkin matured, politically, emotionally, even literarily, over the course of this almost eight-year journey, and his protagonists matured with him. This trip is a universal one: the concerns of a flighty young person (Pushkin? Onegin? You? Me?) seem silly or overwrought and exaggerated by the time we reach our thirties, and if we read *Onegin* slowly we can spend some time thinking about that process of maturation. We can also trace Russia's history in the chapters of the novel—or in what is missing in these chapters.

I talk with students about my favorite Pushkin digressions—I digress all the time in class myself—and they are some of the most charming and insightful aspects of the book. Though Pushkin came to be revered as a Russian literary genius, the digressions show a person who is not at all full of himself, who revels in irony and self-irony. In chapter four, for example, the narrator muses on the process of aging, recalling the joys of champagne (*Veuve Clicquot* or *Moet*): "its magic stream brought forth no end // Of acting foolish, raving madly, // And oh, how many jests and rhymes // And arguments, and happy times!" (Ch. 4, XLV). This merriment, this bubbling over, he implies, is a young person's game. In the next stanza, the poet notes that now he prefers a more prudent *Bordeaux*, a steady friend, to the sparkling mistress, so empty and frivolous. I can't think of another work of world literature where the process of aging is mapped onto the shelves of a wine shop, but it speaks to me—the path from frivolity to pensive contemplation is one I have already traversed. For my students, too, this movement makes sense. Drinkers and teetotalers alike can see that certain patterns—of alcohol consumption, of social behavior— are bound to change with time.

By chapter six the narrator is lamenting that bygone youth: "O dreams! Where has your sweetness vanished? // And where has youth (glib rhyme) been banished?" In Russian the rhyme is *sladost'/ mladost'*—sweetness and youth (Ch. 6, stanza XLIV), and it is as predictable as its English version: vanished/banished. This auto-commentary on his own poetic choices is part of what makes Pushkin's lament so poignant. Soon to turn thirty, the poet recognizes the "midday" of his life and bids his youth farewell. Time marches on, and the poet matures and mellows—and makes fun of his own melancholy with an obvious rhyme, thus downplaying the emotion and poking gentle fun at readers who feel, or anticipate, a similar sadness. We may not be Russian noblemen, but we share a similar fate. No matter our upbringing, the passing of time makes most of us introspective.

Russians have been known to memorize the entire novel, and their slow, careful poring over the pages allows them to delight in the descriptions, those hidden wisdoms, the interactions of narrator with his characters and his readers, the artful rhythms and careful rhymes. *Onegin* is still an escape for Russian readers. For instance, I was surprised to hear a listener's letter read on a Russian literary podcast that detailed how much joy she was getting out of rereading *Onegin* in the summer of 2022—during the Russian war on Ukraine. For her, Pushkin was not an imperialist. He was a haven in a world gone mad.

Pushkin literally plays with his words—which is why he did not write a straightforward prose novel. Rather he invented something that came to be called the "Onegin stanza"—fourteen lines modelled on the sonnet but with a deliberately difficult rhyme scheme that requires significant skill to repeat stanza after stanza, chapter after chapter. Pushkin wrote hundreds of these sonnet-like stanzas, although in his lifetime he wrote very few actual sonnets.

The Onegin stanza is both difficult and fun. My students love to try their hand at it, and though I'm no poet, I admit I've written a few stanzas over the years that I'm even somewhat proud of. In his stanza Pushkin included most of what is feasible in an iambic tetrameter: differing line lengths due to what are called in Russian "masculine" rhymes (i.e., end-stressed) and "feminine" rhymes (with a stress on the penultimate syllable), three different quatrains (alternating rhymes, couplets, "ring" rhymes) and the final rhymed couplet, which can be used to sum up the stanza in an aphoristic way, but—and this is important for the variety of these hundreds of stanzas—does not always do so. The wit and play have to be experienced, and they take the formal qualities of the stanza to a higher level. Trying to write about the rhymes and the playful quality of the narrator's tone is a little like trying to describe the ways a joke is funny. You have to experience it yourself.

I like to explain the stanzaic form to students by saying that it represents an exercise of performing creativity within strict bounds. That is to say, Pushkin's existential dilemma as a Russian nobleman plays out in his verse: he creates for himself specific *poetic* structures that mirror in their way the duties imposed by Russian social structures, and yet he innovates, explores, creates and thus seeks his own inventive path within those limits. The individual in tension with society. Isn't the process of maturation, of leaving behind adolescent ego-centered behavior and thought patterns, precisely about the journey from I to we? Whether we are in alignment with the society in which we live, or in opposition to it, we all must proceed along the path to adulthood and figure out where we stand vis-à-vis larger structures—government, social norms and expectations, and so on. If we find ourselves sipping red wine or fine tea as we age and mellow, we can count ourselves lucky. Pushkin's generation experienced drama.

December 1825: "Time out of Joint"

As Yuri Tynianov would write a century later "In a freezing cold square in the month of December 1825, the people of the twenties, those with a spring in their step, ceased to exist." When in 1825 Tsar Alexander I died unexpectedly, the Russian officers and noblemen who had been gathering for a number of years in so-called secret societies staged a revolt to force the new tsar to permit a constitution, hoping to shift the balance of power from Russia's autocratic system to something more liberal and more democratic. The revolt, led by army officers, was immediately crushed.

Pushkin did not belong to any of the secret societies, but he had gone to school with some of those behind what became known as the "Decembrist Revolt." Pushkin's friends and classmates—including poets Konstantin Ryleev and Wilhelm Kuchelbeker—were punished, either executed or exiled to far-away Siberia, and for him the world seemed to have shifted on its axis. For those "people of the twenties," the world was never the same. In Russia in 1825, time was shattered. And literary plans had to be shifted to fit the new circumstances.

When the atmosphere in Russia underwent a sudden barometric shift—when rebelling officers were arrested and exiled or hanged—Pushkin's Eugene, and the social scene Pushkin had begun to describe in 1823, had to change as well. Over the next five years the poet continued the composition, following his characters and resolving some of their fates, but he slowed and even stopped time, deliberately not allowing the narrative present to reach December 1825. Writing about the Decembrists would have imploded the novel's plot from the inside. In an era of tsarist censorship, it would also have made it unpublishable.

That holding back, that deceleration, makes the novel's internal time even more interesting for the reader. Already a novel of digressions, *Onegin* folds back on itself, with missing stanzas and occasional lack of formal perfection only serving to highlight the structure of the novel and the contradictions of the society it describes. In the very last stanza of chapter eight, Pushkin—in his role as narrator—thinks back to the novel's beginning, remembering those to whom he had read the first verses of chapter one. "Some are no more, and others (are) distant." Among these he might have had in mind Alexander Griboedov—the poet about whom Tynianov wrote the novel I quoted from earlier—who had been arrested during the Decembrist investigations but ultimately died in 1829 as a tsarist official sent to Teheran. Griboedov was not exiled as a punishment, but he was sent on a diplomatic mission that was doomed from the start.

Here in his necessarily cryptic fashion Pushkin is recalling those who perished or suffered at the hands of the tsarist reprisal. When we think about lost and deceased friends, classmates, comrades, we too feel time's momentum even more intensely. This experience is both hugely time-and-place specific and, like most great literature, to use the word I cannot get my students to excise from their active vocabulary, eminently "relatable."

Pushkin himself was never in any real danger from the tsarist regime. He committed no crimes and stirred up no resistance to the government, not really. But in the last six lines of the novel, we sense a moment of survivor guilt:

> But blest is he who rightly gauges
> The time to quit the feast and fly,
> Who never drained life's chalice dry,
> Nor read its novel's final pages,
> But all at once for good withdrew
> As I from my Onegin do.

According to Pushkin, life is a feast, a goblet of wine, a novel to be read and tossed aside. Or perhaps he wished it would be so. He conjured up a set of characters and set them in motion, claiming that life resembles a novel, but as with most Russian fiction to follow, Pushkin does not give his work a happy ending.

Instead, he concludes *Eugene Onegin* abruptly, choosing not to stay to the bitter end of the party. Walking away before the tragedy of December 1825, Pushkin left his readers hanging. It's a perfectly Romantic ending—and it also solves a very real chronological problem for its author. *Eugene Onegin* is more than Romantic. In the relationship that develops between the author and his readers, *Onegin* also becomes a work of realism.

Form and Content

In his 1918 essay "Art as Device," the Russian Formalist critic Viktor Shklovsky wrote, "the goal of art is to create the sensation of seeing, and not merely recognizing, things; the device of art is the "enstrangement" of things and the complication of the form, which increases the duration and complexity of perception, as the process of perception is, in art, an end in itself and must be prolonged."

We've experienced this, and we do so with Pushkin. Any "complication of the form," a form that forces us to acknowledge and notice it, slows down our perception. And that's art, not just fiction. In contrast, reading a mass market paperback I will skip over details, sentences, whole paragraphs, because I want to find out who killed the victim, whether the hero will escape, how many bodies will pile up. That's a different kind of reading. The quantity of dead bodies does not make it a book I will remember or one I will return to.

Instead, if we slow down and read every word, sometimes going back to reread a sentence or a description or a funny way of putting something, we are noticing, interacting with, truly enjoying a novel. And when that novel is a novel-in-verse, the rhymes and even the way the words fill up the lines become part of the pleasure. We are caught up in the descriptions, the form, the foreign culture. We perceive the work in new ways.

What about that plot, though? As my students just begin to get into *Onegin*, they tend to come to class and say: so the guy is a jerk, and he rejects the girl, and then she moves on, and then he wants her? Isn't this just a saga of unrequited love or—to say it in the vernacular— just plain bad timing? Yes, it is. But the form, the "complicated form," makes it so much more.

When asked the definition of a novel, Pushkin once said: *boltovnya*. Chatter. What he meant was that the language of fiction had to mimic that language that spills out of us in friendly conversation. He may have had this idea in part due to his own reading, particularly of epistolary novels, where one person pours out his or her heart to another in letter form. As a keen correspondent, he knew those rhythms. He was also deliberately borrowing literary conventions from other parts of the world and bringing them into the Russian sphere, playing with them, turning them this way and that as he did so.

Why does the non-Russian-speaking reader care? Well, for one, through "chatter" we come to know people, and characters, intimately. This is part of why we love fiction—it takes us into another world, and often into someone else's drawing room, boudoir, garden. The intimacy Pushkin fashions with the reader makes *us* part of the creative process. In reading verse dialogue and descriptions, it is as if we too are speaking in verse, becoming co-creators of the world of the novel. We, like Pushkin, create poetry out of the stuff of everyday life.

But no one speaks in verse, right? Throughout his novel, although he introduces various prose elements into the text, Pushkin deliberately foregrounds the verse, using his stanzas to comment on many situations, whether his own age or biographical circumstances, the fashions and customs of Russians in the city and the countryside, or even the travel conditions in Russia. In so doing, he is also commenting on poetry itself. In verse his commentaries gain weight, become more noticeable, maybe even smarter and more perceptive. In chapter seven, for example, Pushkin's narrator goes on a small diatribe about travel—roads, hotels, and so on (stanzas XXXIII–XXXIV). Poor travel conditions in a foreign land are merely inconvenient, but in one's homeland they are frustrating and embarrassing. This existential problem—Russia as backwater, not-ready-for-European-prime-time—doesn't negate the fact that good travel makes bad stories, and bad travel makes good stories. The details of road conditions or railway sidings or bedbugs in a hotel mattress are grim in the experience, but great in the retelling.

Thus, just as form and content are intrinsically related, I would argue that even as Pushkin's novel foregrounds structure in the novel, it's also about infrastructure. On the face of it tourism and infrastructure don't seem at all poetic, indeed the opposite ... but when we read the particulars in Pushkin's novel, they are revelatory and downright funny. Pushkin asserts that Russian roads will improve in about five hundred years. After my travels across far-flung parts of the Russian empire, I have to agree. Only three hundred more to wait.

The contrasts—verse and prose, city and country, east and west—make the novel worth savoring. Stories require patience, and though Pushkin has invited us along on the journey, he also wants us to experience travelling Russian-style, when you might actually be trapped at an inn by an unexpected cholera outbreak, or by a lack of post-horses, or by roads turned to mud in rainy weather. The personal intonation brings us into the work, and Pushkin plays tricks on his reader, daring us to notice. When his heroine Tatiana falls onto a bench from one stanza into another, we laugh at the stanza break while sharing her chagrin at not being taken seriously as a love interest for Eugene. When the narrator claims boredom and other obligations and leaves us hanging at the end of a chapter, we recall that the novel was serialized. We can just turn the page. Pushkin's contemporaries waited weeks or months to find out "what comes next."

It's a Road Novel: Birth to Death—or Something More Interesting

Many books—novels, short stories, even plays—narrate or stage a set of events. In a biography we expect that we will learn something about the subject's parents and circumstances, about his or her birth, education, adult years, decline, and death. Or in a love story two people meet and their relationship develops, maybe toward a happy ending, maybe toward the death of one person, betrayal, or some other tragic denouement. In a death story—like Tolstoy's *The Death of Ivan Ilych*—we get much of that birth-to-death narrative arc, but with the order mixed up. A book can start with death, or with birth, but we come to expect that we will get to know the characters and watch them develop and change.

The form of the German *Bildungsroman*—popular in Russia, England, France, Germany, and the United States in the nineteenth century—focuses in on just one part of that birth-to-death cycle, the "education" phase, as the young (usually) man who is the hero of the tale leaves adolescence for the complexities of an adult life and absorbs lessons along the way, from books and teachers, of course, but mostly from adventures and interactions with other characters.

One delightful Russian novel with this format is *A Common Story* (1847) by Ivan Goncharov, his debut novel that details the coming-of-age and disillusionment of a young man from the country who embarks upon city life with high hopes and is sorely disappointed. Dostoevsky's *Crime and Punishment* (1865) is a *Bildungsroman* along those same lines: Rodion Raskolnikov comes from a provincial town into the city seeking an education and a leg up. Unlike his French or even English counterparts, or Goncharov's Alexander Aduev, Raskolnikov is not seduced by girls, gossip or greed. Instead, he succumbs to intellectual intoxication and comes to believe in the superior power of the mind, indeed of his own mind, becoming convinced he can use his rational abilities to make his mark on the world. Novelists in the twentieth century continued to write this kind of book. We could call Nabokov's novel *Luzhin's Defense* (1930) a parody of the *Bildungsroman*.

But *Eugene Onegin* opens with the curses of a callow young man: "The devil take you, uncle, die!" Imagining his fate as future caretaker to a shut-in—the uncle whose heir he is has called him to his sickbed—the society fellow does not hesitate to show his disdain for human life. This trajectory from city to country is both the opposite of a *Bildungsroman* and its inversion. If many young people learn from books as well as experience, we are not privileged to watch Onegin learn. Rather than gradually maturing, Eugene is humiliated by the life experiences he has over the course of the novel. More importantly, his internal life is hidden from us, the readers, masked by his *ennui* and posturing. We want him to be a fully fleshed out psychological character, but he remains a caricature. Finally, in chapter seven, the young Tatiana gets access to Onegin's library and pursues her prey from volume to volume:

> Some pages still preserved the traces
> Where fingernails had sharply pressed;
> The girl's attentive eye embraces
> These lines more quickly than the rest.
> And Tanya sees with trepidation
> The kind of thought or observation
> To which Eugene paid special heed,
> Or where he'd tacitly agreed.
> And in the margins she inspected
> His pencil marks with special care;
> And on those pages everywhere
> She found Onegin's soul reflected –
> In crosses or a jotted note,
> Or in the question mark he wrote. (Ch. 7, XXIII)

Noting where he has left his marks on the pages, Tatiana comes to the conclusion that it is not clothes that make the man but his reading list.

By that time in the book, Pushkin's reader has beaten Tatiana to that conclusion. First of all, we've watched Tatiana fall in love with the mysterious Onegin, tracing the steps she knew so well from the novels she herself read. We've mocked her father along with Pushkin's narrator, who tells us of that kindly and distracted man "But still, in books he saw no harm" (Ch. 2, XXIX). We've reminded ourselves to monitor our own children's reading, to be aware of how fiction can shape worldviews and influence expectations. Maybe we've even reflected on how as adults we came to understand our own childhood misapprehensions through the narrative patterns our reading had imprinted on us. Scholars have subjected Tatiana to this test, looking at how Pushkin shows her to be what she has read, how her character was shaped by the literature she preferred—and how perhaps her father should have paid more attention to the effect her reading might have on her.

Secondly, though, we have been encouraged to think about reading habits by the way Pushkin's novel is framed. In the mid-eighteenth century, novels often used elaborate chapter titles to lure us into the thick of things or to help us see what is what. In Henry Fieldings's *Tom Jones* (1749), for example, the title of Book I Chapter IX explains: "Containing matters which will surprise the reader," while Book I Chapter XI's title reads: "Containing many rules, and some examples, concerning falling in love: descriptions of beauty, and other more prudential inducements to matrimony." By the end of that century, novelists were more likely to preface each chapter with an epigraph, and that was the tradition that Pushkin followed. His epigraphs teach his readers the lesson Tatiana learns in Onegin's library, or that we learn from parsing Tatiana's behavior: a (wo)man is what (s)he reads.

Epigraphs are used to set a tone for a novel or a chapter, and to comment on or sum up the contents of what is to come, though more cryptically than an eighteenth-century chapter title. In Pushkin, each epigraph channels a fellow poet, whether the fourteenth-century Italian Petrarch of sonnet fame or Pushkin's personal friends and contemporaries, like Prince Vyazemsky or poet-diplomat Alexander Griboedov. And each epigraph demonstrates Pushkin's erudition, his knowledge of writers from English, French, Italian and Latin traditions as well as Russian, drawing on poets and writers "from Romulus to our days" (Ch. 1, VI).

While setting the tone for the chapter, each epigraph also offers its own tidbit of wisdom. Here we are travelling through the author's reading habits, but in a less haphazard way than via the towering stack of books on a bedside table that we talked about in the introduction. From almost the first line of *Onegin*, we are thinking about time, about young people and about a road they are on. The epigraph from Vyazemsky (Ch. 1) reads "He's hurrying to live and rushing to feel." Pushkin's pace evokes that frenetic careening of youth—and almost immediately we hear Onegin lamenting his fate in a carriage on the way to his uncle's estate. For chapter three, we experience another stereotype about young people, this one about women. Pushkin quotes Malfilâtre in French: "She was young, she was [likely to fall] in love." Because this "she" (like the "he" in Vyazemsky) is general, it helps Pushkin make Tatiana a "type," representing young women of her class and time, even as she is particular and specific, her own individual with feelings and thoughts. Later he highlights how much Tatiana loves the countryside and winter, traits he ties to "Russianness." Petrarch (cited in Italian as the epigraph to chapter six) offers another view into what it means to be Russian: "There, where the days are cloudy and short / Is born a race that has no fear of death." The reference is to Russian bravado and the nobility's habit of fighting duels, and instead of paying them a compliment, it seems the southern poet is maligning the Russians along with their climate. Pushkin, though, shows his erudition: his epigraphs in many languages identify him as a man of the world, even if he does all his traveling within the Russian empire.

The Novel (and Love) as Deceit

The Russian language takes its word for long form fiction, *roman*, from the French word for novel. And as in French, *roman* can also mean a love affair. The fact that there are often love intrigues in a novel gives a logic to this homonymic situation, and for Pushkin it also offers yet another opportunity for play.

In chapter three of *Eugene Onegin*, Pushkin pokes fun at the concept of the novel in European literature. His heroine, Tatiana Larina, has fallen in love with Eugene, and she sees in him not a human being, but a composite character from the fiction she has read: Grandison from Richardson's *Clarissa* (1748), Rousseau's Wolmar (1761), Goethe's Werther (originally 1774), Julie de Krüdener's de Linar (1804) and Sophie Cottin's hero Malek Adhel (1805). This idea, of a young woman getting to know the parameters of relationships with the opposite sex through reading fiction, makes the novel a metatext. Tatiana, a "young dreamer," merges all the examples of possible lovers in one and imagines that Onegin shares their characteristics. But she is mistaken. Pushkin's narrator tells us: "Her hero ... was none the less // No Grandison in Russian dress" (Ch. 3, X).

Pushkin is writing not just about how young people come to understand the world, in this case through imaginative literature. He is also explaining the connection between fictional plots and the narrative of life: if fiction is drawn from life, life too imitates fiction. Reading is a source of information, understanding, emotion, but it can also be dangerous. When we expect the world to mirror what we've read, we can misinterpret life's situations.

In chapter two, introducing us to Tatiana, Pushkin's narrator had said: "From early youth she read romances, // And novels set her heart aglow; // She loved the fictions and the fancies // Of Richardson and of Rousseau" (Ch. 2, XXIX). Tatiana's father, the narrator explains, was not a reader. But Pushkin codified that danger with his own rhyme: *romany / obmany*—novels and deceits (the translator uses the word "romances" for "novels" to avoid ambiguity). Women, the novel seems to argue, generally manipulate men's feelings, pulling them in, pushing them away and then reeling them back in again. They are inherently deceitful as they play games of love. However, Pushkin's own heroine is sweet and innocent. He shows her reacting to a man who does not exist, wanting to be the heroine of a novel (which, in fact, she is). But then he must bring her down ... and in so doing, sharing the letter she writes Onegin on the model of all those letters in the English and French epistolary novels she so loves, he plays again with his rhymes. Now "Tatiana" is brought into a rhymed pair with *obmana*, deceit. According to the narrator, the heroine with "her simple heart," "trusting," "warm and tender," "in deceit will take no part" (Ch. 3,

XXIV). But rhymed with deceit, is she tainted? Pushkin protects her in the end, enabling her to steel her heart and make rational choices to value her honor—her pledge upon giving her word in marriage to be true to her husband—over love. In the existential quandary, duty wins over desire. But she might have made another choice.

In chapter four, when the novel's second protagonist, the young poet Vladimir Lensky, sits musing on his future with his own beloved (Tatiana's sister Olga), Pushkin uses this same rhyme, *roman / obman*, novel (love affair) and deceit. To fully live our lives, the narrator suggests, we must be open to being deceived, to being fooled. That is an essential and pleasurable part of the trip.

> Yes, he was loved … beyond deceiving …
> Or so at least with joy he thought.
> Oh, blest is he who lives believing,
> Who takes cold intellect for naught,
> Who rests within the heart's sweet places
> As does a drunk in sleep's embraces,
> Or as, more tenderly I'd say,
> A butterfly in blooms of May;
> But wretched he who's too far-sighted,
> Whose head is never fancy-stirred,
> Who hates all gestures, each warm word,
> As sentiments to be derided,
> Whose heart … experience has cooled
> And barred from being loved … or fooled! (Ch. 4, LI)

Eugene, the "hero" of the novel, in the narrator's estimation is *wretched*. Unable to believe or to be fooled, he misses out on love until it is too late. In contrast, though the poet Lensky is foolish, he is at least happy. Even if he *isn't* really loved, if he's only deceiving himself, he is *blest* rather than *wretched*. Pushkin used this technique of contrasting his heroes (or heroines, as in Tatiana and Olga), but he also made it very clear which path is more appealing.

And here we see that this novel, this *roman*, acts just as a love relationship does. The genre of the novel requires that we throw ourselves into it, that we suspend disbelief and allow ourselves to experience the words and sentiments of the characters, follow along with the plot as it unfolds. As Nabokov has argued, we must become good readers and open ourselves to the fiction. We embrace deception, the author's deception. That same capacity, Pushkin asserted, is necessary to live a happy life.

In creating this "novel-in-verse," Pushkin was leaving behind the jaded Byronic hero and striving toward a more genuine character. Here, in the closing lines of the first half of the novel, Pushkin suggested that it's okay to be fooled. We ought to descend into that world of deceit, similar if not identical to the world of imagination. Even if disappointment or death await us—and they do, inevitably, as often in life as in fiction—the journey merits the price. Ennui, a jaded, cynical attitude toward life, may look cool in a Byronic or James Dean kind of way, but Pushkin here suggests that looking cool is not worth it. Rather enthusiasm and imagination, allowing ourselves to be fooled, enables us to authentically experience emotion, passion, love. Better a fool than a cool dude. Because the cool dude always ends up alone.

In Pushkin's novel, the cool dude, Onegin, plays a more sinister part—he steps into the role of a stone-cold killer. In a petulant reaction to Lensky's jealousy that Onegin was flirting with his beloved Olga, Onegin accepts the younger man's challenge, and they proceed to duel. Readers watch in horror as the two enter into a game of chicken and, as with James Dean in *Rebel without a Cause*, Eugene kills his friend. My students are amazed that Pushkin predicted his own death by duel (and sometimes they wonder why *so* many Russian authors engaged in duels). I have to remind them that while Pushkin initiated more than a dozen duels and participated in almost twenty, he also knew that the honor code in Russia did not require murder. He avoided bloodshed—until 1837, when he became its victim. By commenting on dueling in *Onegin*, Pushkin emphasized its ritual aspects and highlighted its fratricidal potential. For younger readers, the novel is a love story, but for more mature ones it points to the stupidity of young men and the reckless impulses they cannot control.

The End of the Journey

Let's pause just for a moment at the very end of the novel. In point of fact, it really is a "road novel," one in which we follow Pushkin's characters from city to countryside to Moscow and back to Petersburg, to the shores of the Neva River "where maybe, reader, you began," as the narrator initially addresses his audience (Ch. 1, II). Missing from the novel are the years Pushkin planned to show his hero Onegin *actually travelling*. When his protagonist arrives back in St. Petersburg from his self-imposed exile after killing Lensky, the narrator quotes from another famous text about a travelling hero, Griboedov's play *Woe from Wit*, saying that Onegin has arrived (as if) "from a ship directly to the ball." Because of this it seems to us that Onegin has just returned from a grand European tour. In fact, the missing bits and stanzas, sometimes collected as "Onegin's Journey," show us that he went to Odessa, to the steppe and to other parts of the Russian empire, and like his creator Pushkin never left its confines.

In the last stanzas that Pushkin did include in the novel, we see something else: journey—and feast, and drink, and fiction—as metaphor. Let's look again at those last six lines of chapter eight:

> But blest is he who rightly gauges
> The time to quit the feast and fly,
> Who never drained life's chalice dry,
> Nor read its novel's final pages,
> But all at once for good withdrew
> As I from my Onegin do.

If in the middle of the novel it is the poet Lensky who is "blest," who feels love because he can believe in passion and honor and friendship, now the narrator wants to claim that "blest" status for himself by walking away midstream. Romantic poetry values the fragment, and here the narrative ends abruptly, with no real conclusion. It is a true Romantic poem, despite the "devil of a difference" Pushkin claimed by writing a *novel* in verse.

What does that say to us as people who read life as a journey, who read a feast as a party with a beginning *and* an ending, who generally enjoy a novel that comes to a conclusion rather than a sudden end? And why would we return to this novel, again and again, as Russian and other readers continue to do? One place we might find our answers is in Pushkin's historical circumstances. Pushkin was born in the era of Alexander I which began as a relatively benign time. Under Nicholas I the tsarist regime took another repressive turn, and Pushkin's novel reflects the tragedy that was the Decembrist revolt. In his novel Pushkin employed a deceleration of time, slowing down so as not to reach 1825, and that enabled him to avoid confronting and coming to terms with the arrests of those implicated in the revolt or in ideas that led to revolt, or with the deaths of his friends and classmates punished for their freethinking.

A novel with no ending, a life with no death—that is the journey that Pushkin seems to evoke in his work. And the calculation—*blest is he who rightly gauges*—the proper timing, the clever approach to life, here replaces the "deceit" that is falling in love. We throw ourselves into life, fools in love, and yet … Pushkin tells us to hold back, to step away before it is too late. This novel with its relatively simple plot actually holds a lot of clues: to complex historical situations, to the role of literary history, to a philosophy of life in constrained circumstances. It lives up to its elaborate design, and we find ourselves wanting to slow down, to pause and think, and to consider rereading.

CHAPTER 3
LARGER THAN LIFE: LEO
TOLSTOY'S WORLD

When she thought of Vronsky, she imagined that he did not love her, that he was already beginning to be burdened by her, that she could not offer herself to him, and she felt hostile to him because of it. It seemed to her that the words she had spoken to her husband, and which she kept repeating in her imagination, had been spoken to everyone and that everyone had heard them. She could not bring herself to look into the eyes of those she lived with. She could not bring herself to call her maid and still less to go downstairs to see her son and the governess. (*Anna Karenina*)

When I think of Tolstoy, I love to imagine him as Christopher Plummer played him in the film *The Last Station* (2009): hearty, ardent, roaring with laughter. But he was not only that big passionate person. He was also reflective, self-doubting, quick to anger, eager to invent ways to deny his own desires. In that sense, he was not dissimilar to his heroine Anna Karenina, whose thoughts we see in the text cited above, or indeed to her foil in the novel of that name, Konstantin Levin.

Of the authentic Russian "greats," no one brings in as many readers as Lev, in common English usage Leo, Tolstoy, who lived the longest of any of them, from 1828 to 1910. That long life allowed Tolstoy to have a vast array of experiences across the Russian empire, including in the Caucasus where he started his literary career in two genres: dispatches from the front and autobiography. His first two works were the so-called *Sevastopol Sketches* and the trilogy *Childhood. Boyhood. Youth* and though based on his experiences, both were fictionalized. They offered observations into what would become Tolstoy's favorite realms: the heightened experiences of war and of the "other," and the home front—family, city life, the Russian country estate. Though the narrative stance in these early works mirrored his own position as a privileged scion of a wealthy family, he would eventually expand to write from various points of view, including those of a young woman, a simple peasant, a dog, and a horse. In creating his fictional characters, Tolstoy drew on history and his own biography, and he recombined the traits of real people in his life. The vivid nature of those characters resonates for readers, and their contradictions give us license to feel changeable ourselves.

During his lifetime Tolstoy's estate south of Tula, called Yasnaya Polyana, became a pilgrimage site, and his oft-reproduced portraits remind us that the old man resembled a prophet. He is almost the axiomatic Russian writer: long flowing beard, idiosyncratic personal habits (made his own boots, drank mare's milk, was a vegetarian, eschewed tobacco and alcohol, founded his own religion), even had an aristocratic title ("Count"). Tolstoy was larger than life, and his work reflects that fact. Many of his books run to numerous volumes.

But the Russia Tolstoy described is long gone. His princesses at debutante balls and dashing hussars on horseback, his peasants patiently cultivating the land, his servant women enduring the unwanted sexual attention of their masters, evoke another world. Why do readers continue to flock to his writing? Using *Anna Karenina*, one of the most beloved but also most accessible of his novels, this chapter considers how the experience of reading that novel changes over time and why it is worth going back to. Personally and in the classroom, I've found that I can return to *Anna* again and again, always finding something new, and always marveling over what Tolstoy called the *architectonics* of the novel, the intricate and rewarding structure of the plot. But even as the aesthetics of the form give an underlying satisfaction, the individual pieces of any narrative must also appeal to the reader. And the stories of how the novel's two protagonists Anna and Levin seek happiness and the meaning of life through all manner of complications remain appealing.

This is what draws me to Russian literature and to great literature more generally: authors' ambitions in tackling big questions—everything from birth, illness, and death to love, faithfulness, and family to spirituality, aesthetics, and war—and their skill in organizing them into narrative, telling stories that illuminate and investigate the questions that matter most in life. Though easily lampooned by cartoonists, other authors, and filmmakers (like Woody Allen in his 1975 film *Love and Death*), Tolstoy's explorations of nineteenth-century families in the city and countryside, his search for moral guidelines and principles by which to live life, his portrayals of such varied topics as haymaking and provincial political processes, breastfeeding and horseracing, restaurant culture and jam-making, religion and philosophy, mean that *Anna Karenina* teems with characters who seem real and who confront real-life problems while they engage in everyday behaviors.

Not every page is compelling to every age, but it strikes me that eventually they will all resonate with most readers. Only recently, for example, did the agricultural and political reforms described in such detail in the second half of the novel really grab my attention. (In fact, I used to recommend that students who are short on time skip these passages. I still make that suggestion—but then I remind students that it is precisely these pages that they may come back to when electoral politics or sustainable farming practices feel more relevant to their lives.) Other things that once seemed alien have since become part of my own experience. Tolstoy's death scenes have become more compelling; childbirth and the fear for children's welfare and development are already very real to me, and the loss of loved ones to disease and accident is real as well. The marital relations seemed foreign to me as a college student, but now those conversations make much more sense, and I even love Tolstoy's big "how to have a happy marriage" takeaway—one that draws on his own courtship but surely did not work for him in the long run. The skill of "wordless communication" is something that my husband and I continue to hone, and joke about, on a daily basis.

Anna Karenina and other such vibrant novels warrant rereading, and many people admit to rereading Tolstoy, some every year, in a ritualistic kind of way. Others turn to Tolstoy's *War and Peace* or *Anna Karenina* in their later years, upon discovering a feeling that they are ready for the experience, or in wartime—scholars have documented how during the Second World War soldiers and civilians alike sought out copies of *War and Peace*, and during the current Russian war on Ukraine I have heard the same.

As Nabokov argued, rereading is as important as reading. David Herman, a professor of Russian literature at the University of Virginia, calls himself a "serial rereader" of *Anna Karenina*, and I guess as college instructors we are all serial rereaders, always brushing up each time we teach a work of literature again and often actually rereading every page of the novels and short stories alongside our students. I find that if I don't have time to reread—if other obligations somehow get in the way—my teaching is not as fresh, my reactions and readings not as strong. But the more I revisit a novel or other work of literature, the more I want to share it—with students, with family, with friends. This affords me an intimate relationship of my own with the actual text, with a description or a character or a chapter beginning or ending. I love to experience this literature, paragraph by paragraph, page by page, and to observe how I read it differently each time.

In Tolstoy's sprawling novels, the huge number of characters, all of whom have three or four forms of their name, can be frustrating for a lay reader, but their presence also creates a feeling of verisimilitude: the world is large, and most of us encounter many individuals over the course of a day, a week, a lifetime. If each individual has an internal world, then our own experiences and sensations gain additional meaning, validity, affirmation. Tolstoy is one of those writers who remind us that we inhabit our own worlds and can have a hard time seeing into the inner lives of others. He shows us how.

The Structure of the Novel

On January 27, 1878, Tolstoy wrote to retired Moscow University botany professor S. A. Rachinsky in response to the latter's assessment of *Anna Karenina*. Rachinsky—who, like Tolstoy, had taken up teaching peasant children in a country school—praised *Anna* as Tolstoy's best work yet, but he found it to have a "basic deficiency in

[its] construction." In his view, there were two themes developed side by side in the novel, but the writer had failed to connect them in any way. Tolstoy disagreed.

> Your opinion about *Anna Karenina* does not seem correct to me. On the contrary, I take pride in the architectonics. The vaults are done in such a way that one cannot even notice the place where they are linked. I took more care in that than in anything else. The unification of the structure is rendered not by action and not by the relationships of characters, but by an inner connection. Believe me, this is not a lack of willingness to accept criticism, especially from you whose opinion is always excessively generous, but I am afraid that reading through the novel, you did not notice its inner content.

This word, "architectonics," refers to the structure of a musical, literary, or artistic work, but we see that Tolstoy has an almost physical notion of his novel as a piece of architecture. As with a medieval cathedral, the novel would collapse if any one piece were to be removed. Strength and support are built into its very structure. Tolstoy was adamant about the "inner content" of his work, rejecting the misreading of even a perceptive friend.

Rachinsky may have been led astray by that most quoted sentence from Tolstoy, the very first sentence of the novel: "All happy families resemble one another but each unhappy family is unhappy in its own way." As we begin the novel, it seems like we will have two families, each of which belongs to one of these categories. If Anna's marriage is doomed and her fate sad, as we will learn by the end of the novel, then surely her family is the "unhappy one," which makes the other "line" of the novel the "happy" one—Levin and his eventual bride Kitty. But this sentence, as brilliantly formulated as it is and as memorable, tricks us into binary thinking that is both highly Tolstoyan and also anti-Tolstoyan.

Let me explain what I mean by this. As I've indicated earlier, the vast cast of characters in many a Tolstoy novel helps us to understand that the world is populated by people of different kinds. Tolstoy wants *complexity* in his people. He is not content to have all army officers be straight out of Central Casting; instead, he gives us three, or five, or half a dozen army officers, each with his own idiosyncrasies. This is why I say that binary thinking is anti-Tolstoyan. If everything in life is either black or white, either zero or one—to speak the language of computers—that is rather dull. Tolstoy did not think life was predictable, nor that it should be portrayed that way. On the other hand, in Tolstoy's world many binaries were quite relevant: young people act one way, the older generation another; men have certain obligations, and women others; servants cannot move into upper echelons, and those from the nobility who descend in social rank are violating their birthright and all sense of propriety. Tolstoy portrays Levin's brother Nikolai doing just that, and his reader senses how wrong such behavior is.

One of the classic ways to look at Tolstoy is to ask, as Isaiah Berlin did in a famous essay entitled "The Hedgehog and the Fox" (1953), which of these creatures the author might resemble. "A fox knows many things, but a hedgehog knows one big thing," the Greek philosopher Archilochus supposedly wrote. Tolstoy, Berlin eventually argues, was a fox by nature but a hedgehog by conviction. I suppose that idea confirms my own take, that both binaries and a resistance to binaries characterize Tolstoy's thinking.

Let's return to that first line of *Anna Karenina*: "All happy families resemble one another but each unhappy family is unhappy in its own way." The more you read it over, the more you wonder whether it is even true. Could it be, rather, that all unhappy families resemble each other, while all happy families are different? Or could it be that *all* families resemble each other? Or that *no* family resembles any other? What was Tolstoy saying with that opening line? In a way he was challenging us: are we binary thinkers? Are we seeking rules and regulations of behavior, are we trying to characterize and pigeonhole people we meet and read about? Or are we open to changing perspectives?

Although there are two main plots in the novel, the Anna plot and the Levin plot, there are many more families, and in characteristically perverse fashion, Tolstoy begins the novel with yet a third family. *Anna Karenina* is about infidelity, as most readers today who are aware of the basics of the novel know. But the infidelity in the opening pages was not performed by the title character. The second sentence of the novel reads "Everything was upset in the Oblonsky household."

Thus the novel's structure, or the "vaults" as Tolstoy calls them, is reinforced through family (Anna is Stiva Oblonsky's sister, and her home in St. Petersburg is connected with his in Moscow) and through affinity (Anna is a wife who can try to advise Stiva's betrayed wife Dolly; Dolly is a sister to Kitty, the young girl who has fallen in love with Count Vronsky; Vronsky himself will quickly begin to fall for Anna, which will intensify Kitty's feelings for both when she realizes it; Anna judges her brother for his infidelity and then will herself take steps down that path). Within these relationships Tolstoy also connects characters through similarity and contrast. Dolly is the deceived wife, her sister the ingenue. Kitty feels compromised by Vronsky, and Anna does as well when he makes advances while knowing she is a married woman. These links continue throughout the novel, through blood, social affinity, and personal affection or irritation. But Tolstoy claimed in his letter to Rachinsky that the links are not merely about action or the relationships among characters. We need to continue seeking the hidden "inner content" about which he speaks.

Descriptions and Details

The reader has to wait to meet the novel's title character. A telegram introduces her in chapter two as one who may reconcile the unhappy spouses, but Anna herself does not appear until chapter eighteen. Those who are surprised that Mikhail Bulgakov does not bring his hero, the Master, into *Master and Margarita* until chapter thirteen, or that Margarita arrives even later in the novel, would do well to remember their Tolstoy. In *Anna Karenina*, the wait is worth it. Seen through the eyes of Count Alexei Vronsky, the "lady" is striking, and after she passes he feels the need to look at her one more time:

> not because she was very beautiful, not because of the elegance and modest grace that could be seen in her whole figure, but

because there was something especially gentle and tender in the expression of her sweet-looking face as she stepped past him. … Her shining grey eyes, which seemed dark because of their thick lashes, rested amiably and attentively on his face, as if she recognized him … . In that brief glance, Vronsky had time to notice the restrained animation that played over her face and fluttered between her shining eyes and the barely noticeable smile that curved her red lips. It was as if a surplus of something so overflowed her being that it expressed itself beyond her will, now in the brightness of her glance, now in her smile. She deliberately extinguished the light in her eyes, but it shone against her will in a barely noticeable smile.

Face, eyes, lips. Vronsky's gaze moves along this trajectory four times, and the reader's with his. Anna—not yet identified—is elegant and graceful, but any woman of her class might seem so. The adjectives—kind, gentle, endearing—suggest she is different, something special. In this description we see Anna's struggle, or what Vronsky perceives to be her struggle, to control her internal life force via her strength of will. In contrast, Countess Vronsky, Alexei's mother, is a "dry old woman" marked by withered features. She "narrows" her eyes and "smiles slightly with her thin lips," offering "her small, dry hand" to her son.

Here is an example of how Tolstoy draws in the reader and carefully links his characters in numerous ways: through (1) physical proximity—Countess Vronsky and Anna have ridden together to Moscow in the same train compartment; (2) affinity—both upper class women, they are also both mothers of sons, and they have spent the trip discussing their boys and their motherly feelings; and (3) bodily traits—eyes, lips. The women are polite with each other. They "connect" through Vronsky. This is only the beginning of their connection, and in time Countess Vronsky will come to wonder at her initial warm feelings toward Anna.

Tolstoy was more than just a chronicler of the society and ideas of his time, more than just a moralist, though in his later years the "prophet" aspect tended to dominate his reputation. First and foremost,

Tolstoy was an artist, and an epic artist at that. So, when critics reduce a novel like *Anna Karenina* to an "encyclopedia of changing attitudes toward women in Russian society of the 1870s," as some have, they are seeing the social trees and missing the enormous forest entirely. *Anna Karenina* participates in the conversations of its place and age, and it reaches across the years to speak to us in our time. Questions of marriage, of family, of the role women play in societies large and small, are as relevant for today's reader as for the Russian reader of the 1870s. In a binary view, Dolly, the quintessential mother, illustrates the negative aspect of the marriage contract that does not bind her husband as tightly, while Anna exemplifies the struggle between the spirit and the flesh. This is overly reductive, of course. We know from our own lives that women are both mothers and human beings, with desires and aspirations that go beyond just fulfilling their children's needs. We watch as characters think about their own requirements, as they try to define the path to a contented life. How to satisfy both aspects within any social contract was a problem in Tolstoy's world and remains a burning issue for women today.

Slowing down to look at details brings issues like these to a simmer as we read the novel, giving us time to think, compare, judge if we so choose. Having examined how Tolstoy introduces his title heroine, let's notice, too, the physical attributes of the youngest heroine, Kitty. An eighteen-year-old girl, recently out in society, she steps onto the grand staircase of her Moscow home where a ball is already underway. Kitty Shcherbatskaya is pink, both because of her "intricate tulle gown over a pink underskirt" and because she is blooming with health and anticipation, her hair piled high and topped with a rose, her neck encircled by a black velvet ribbon. The narrator tells us that Kitty is "having one of her happy days," and we learn that her shoes do not pinch, her dress is not tight anywhere, her long gloves embrace her arms, and "in her bare shoulders and arms she felt a cold, marble-like quality that she especially liked." As in his description of Anna at the railway station, Tolstoy here lingers on the face of his young girl: "her eyes shone, and her red lips could not help smiling from the sense of her own attractiveness." We don't judge her for her youthful vanity but rather are happy for her. We sense her physicality just as Kitty senses the possibilities of the party—indeed, she embodies them, along with the charms of her own outfit, her lightness on her feet. As readers we too feel the joy and the electricity of the evening.

If the women's faces, and their light steps, are the focus of Tolstoy's description and what draws the notice of the reader, the men's facial features also get his attention. Part I of the novel ends with Karenin's big ears and Vronsky's strong teeth. The trip to Moscow has changed Anna, and the men in her life reflect those changes. Perhaps Anna has become more attuned to her surroundings after her trip to try to salvage her brother's marriage, but why has she never noticed those ears before? The everyday aspects of life in St. Petersburg—spending time with her husband's friend, with her son, with her correspondence— bring Anna back to her regular existence after the interlude in Moscow, but she remains puzzled about those ears: "Did he have his hair cut?" We as readers also think about the features that define these men and women. When do we see features on a face: only upon first meeting? When we already have feelings for someone? When do those features become more noticeable, or less? When do they change?

When Vronsky returns to his St. Petersburg lodgings—after declaring to Anna on the railroad platform that his admiration for her does not and will not take her married status into account—he finds his friend and comrade Petritsky with a lady-friend. Here Tolstoy shows infidelity in Petersburg as well, and he also introduces the idea of divorce into the novel. The baroness begins to complain that despite her indiscretions her husband won't release her from her marriage. Characterizing Vronsky's world as "gay and pleasant," "carefree," Tolstoy injects a frivolous, joking tone into this first real scene on Vronsky's home grounds, and in reaction to the stories being told, "Vronsky rocked with laughter," "exposing a solid row of strong teeth." Thus, the binary of Moscow/Petersburg is echoed by the binary of Anna's home and Vronsky's quarters, the first serious and calm with occasional mocking smile or tone on the part of Karenin, and the latter marked by unseriousness, playfulness, merriment. The two worlds will meet in Anna and Vronsky's budding relationship, and Tolstoy's emphasis on Vronsky's strong white teeth finds its echo in the count's love of racehorses and of one in particular, his beloved

Frou-Frou, whose graceful neck resembles, in Tolstoy's telling, the neck of his future mistress.

In Tolstoy's fictional world individuals are important, and so are relationships among them. Families, both happy and unhappy, are central to the narrative. But equally vital is the relationship each individual has with him or herself, with the body. The physicality of Tolstoy's characters mirrors our own experience of our bodies, which may ache or feel strong and exultant. Tolstoy is particularly good with those physical details, and in *Anna* he wields them like a double-edged sword: the details tell us about the person to whom they belong *and* about the person(s) who observe them. They also in some small way make the characters more vivid, more real to the reader, but as they bring us into the novel's action, surrounding us and immersing us, they can also push us to think about the process of reading and of description. Those recurring epithets throw me back to reading *The Odyssey* in high school and being struck by the "fiery-headed Menelaus" and the "rosy fingers of dawn." Vronsky's strong teeth, Anna's delicate neck, Karenin's big ears. Tolstoy uses these markers to draw attention to his characters' traits, to highlight their physicality and their presence in the world.

Characters and Place

These characters do not exist in a vacuum. They exist in space. In the early scenes of the novel, we realize that trains and train stations are places where Anna and others are on display. In the compartment chatting with Countess Vronsky, and later returning to Petersburg, as she reads her English book and gazes out the window, she is being observed, by those around her and by us, Tolstoy's readers. Her manners and mannerisms—the way she removes her gloves, the way she tosses her head, the reticule she holds—tell us that she is a beautiful woman used to being looked at, but also one who is certain that she is protected by her marital status. No one would dare to violate her person, she believes, given her reputation and good standing in society. And yet, the train takes her, rapidly, from one place to another, and when she arrives in Moscow the train station functions as a place that brings varieties of people together and as a stage on which we the readers (and other characters) observe them. The classes mix, or at least occupy the same area, and in that mixing lies danger for Anna. She is seen by Vronsky, his mother, her brother, and others beside. Self-confident from her own womanly point of view, she is nonetheless more vulnerable than she realizes.

The two cities offer a number of spaces where women are seen: on train platforms and in public streets, but also in private salons and living rooms, at theaters, at racetracks. A key moment, in the first part of the novel, is when Anna appears at that very same ball that starts with what Kitty thinks is a "happy day," but that ends in tears and disappointment, even despair for the younger woman. Anna's black velvet gown is lowcut and trimmed in Venetian lace, and her neck is adorned by tendrils of curly black hair. We see her through the young Kitty's eyes, and along with her we recognize that "her loveliness consisted precisely in always standing out from what she wore," the black dress "was just a frame, and only she was seen—simple, natural, graceful, and at the same time gay and animated." Tolstoy will highlight Anna's neck, and those curls, again at other key moments in the novel, but here we watch as Kitty expresses her love for her aunt: gazing at her as if at a portrait but also sensing her move through space. That physicality, and the details of Anna's person, strike Kitty and us readers as well. Kitty finds her to be perfect, "splendid" … until Anna replaces her in the estimation of the man she dreamed of as a suitor, at which point she realizes that "there is something terrible and cruel in her enchantment." Kitty, the fresh rose, has wilted, and her transformation is physical as well as psychological, making her almost unrecognizable.

Display and competition. That's what the Moscow marriage market is all about, and perhaps that is the fate of women more generally—even today. Certainly, when they discuss this topic in class, college students sometimes talk about the "meat markets" they themselves feel subjected to on and off campus. I've had women students complain about being looked at rather than listened to, and men protest that they cannot *not* look if women students insist on wearing clingy tops and short shorts. Could we say about Anna that Vronsky was attracted to her because of the way she was dressed? For Tolstoy that was surely part of it—after all, he got to choose the outfits.

Tolstoy intensifies our reactions to his characters by showing them experiencing themselves—their bodies, their roles, the effect they have on others. And he shows others reacting to them. They become three-dimensional, first because they are visible: to themselves, to other characters, and to readers. But more importantly, when these three-dimensional human beings move through space, sometimes elegantly, as Kitty does gliding across the ice at a Moscow skating rink, and sometimes awkwardly, as Levin when he resolutely refuses to observe the code of behavior at the English Club while dining there with Stiva, they are inhabiting their bodies. Levin's awkwardness is as important as Kitty or Anna's elegance in making us appreciate Tolstoy's art of the body and of the humans that occupy those bodies.

The portrait that Kitty sees, with Anna in its stop-frame, will resonate with other portraits later in the novel—part of Tolstoy's connecting "inner content." But if women were to be seen only, then they would not qualify as complete human beings. Tolstoy shows us the physical specimens, but he makes sure to make them live, to show that they cannot remain in their frames but are destined to burst out of them, to seek motion and change. Tolstoy chronicles the ways in which women dress and perform for those who view them, but he also allows them some autonomy to ignore the gazes constricting them and make their own way in the world, for better or for worse. It is at moments like these when I assert to my students that Tolstoy was a feminist in his way, treating his women characters like real human beings whose thoughts, words, and actions have real-world consequences. He gave them that possibility, he made them real, and of course that also meant that his women (like most of his men) were internally inconsistent, divided in their aims and impulses. They were human.

Biology and Biography

Tolstoy is one of the authors frequently mentioned in the new trend of "life lessons from literature." And not without reason. Tolstoy's epic novels include all possible life experiences, especially death, and birth, and marriage. The relationship of the novel form to biography, though, deserves exploration. Biography literally means "the writing of a life" or "a life written down." With so many characters in Tolstoy's fiction, he cannot follow all of them along that birth-to-death trajectory. What he does do, though, is to give us highlights of each of the major life events across a set of characters, increasing the complexity of the world he portrays while also connecting the human beings who occupy it to each other and potentially to his readers as well.

As a philosophically inclined young man, Tolstoy was always trying to figure out his relationship to the world around him and to the events that occur naturally within it. Death in particular was a terrifying prospect for him, and that perhaps is why he returned to it again and again. In *War and Peace* time slows down when death approaches. In *Anna Karenina* death permeates the room—several times—as well as the consciousness of those who are dying. Since death looms so large in Tolstoy's own consciousness, I'd like to start with that, and we'll move to happier moments later. Not surprisingly—if we remember Tolstoy's "vaults"—death and other life events are frequently connected, which helps to create that hidden inner content of the novel.

Death is present at the railroad station in the very opening pages of the novel, but real worries about death enter the novel *Anna Karenina* when Konstantin Levin's brother Nikolai comes to visit him just as Kostya is planning new efforts on his agricultural estate. Two very important ideas are conveyed in this chapter (XXXI), the last in Part III of the novel. The first has to do with kinship between people who are close, and the other has to do with the inexorable approach of death.

Even before Kostya sees who has arrived unexpectedly to visit him, a cough gives Nikolai away. Kostya's first reaction is disappointment— he had hoped the guest would bring distraction and amusement— but then he is almost immediately overcome with pity. As sometimes happens with siblings, Kostya feels his brother's bodily state almost physically. The narrator takes us into Kostya's mind: "Frightening as his brother Nikolai's thinness and sickliness had been before, he was now still thinner, still more wasted. He was a skeleton covered with skin." Knowing that the two of them should speak freely, that their shared history means they understand each other thoroughly, even without words, Kostya longs to speak the truth to his brother, to talk with him about the death he sees in his every movement, his very corpus:

> These two men were so dear and close to each other that the slightest movement, the tone of the voice, told them both more than it was possible to say in words.
>
> Now they both had one thought—Nikolai's illness and closeness to death—which stifled all the rest. But neither of them dared to speak of it, and therefore everything else they said, without expressing the one thing that preoccupied them, was a lie.

The idea of wordless communication is one that Tolstoy highlights several times in the novel. He believes that when people are truly on one wavelength, when they are meant for each other—whether in love, as Kostya and Kitty, or because of shared history, biography, biology— they do not need to speak in order to understand one another. Here the brothers deliberately lie to each other out loud, and they remain dissatisfied. But as they are parting they manage, through looks and gestures, to say what they mean:

> Only just before his departure Nikolai exchanged kisses with him and said, suddenly giving his brother a strangely serious look:
>
> "Anyhow, don't think badly of me, Kostya!" and his voice trembled.
>
> These were the only sincere words spoken. Levin understood that they implied: "You see and know that I'm in a bad way and we may never see each other again." Levin understood it, and tears gushed from his eyes. He kissed his brother once more, but there was nothing he could or knew how to say to him.

Perfectly healthy himself, Kostya comes to believe through spending time with his brother that he has forgotten the one important thing in life. And this is the other vital idea that Tolstoy conveys here at the end of Part III of his novel: at any moment death can come, and it will come, no matter what. Konstantin Levin is terribly afraid of death, and becoming aware of its possibility shifts the way he looks at the world. He spends an uncomfortable night listening to the tossing and turning of his ill brother:

> Death, the inevitable end of everything, presented itself to him for the first time with irresistible force. And this death, which was here, in his beloved brother, moaning in his sleep and calling by habit, without distinction, now on God, now on the devil, was not at all as far off as it had seemed to him before. It was in him, too—he felt it. If not now, then tomorrow, if not tomorrow, then in thirty years—did it make any difference? And what this inevitable death was, he not only did not know, he not only had never thought of it, but he could not and dared not think of it. … the more he strained to think, the clearer it became to him that it was undoubtedly so, that he had actually forgotten, overlooked in his life one small circumstance—that death would come and everything would end, that it was not worth starting anything and that nothing could possibly be done about it. Yes, it was terrible, but it was so.

Here we might recall that Anna's family was supposed to be the unhappy one! These thoughts tumble pell-mell through Kostya's head, rapidly becoming exaggerated in a way that feels authentic—that kind of overthinking that leads to a hysterical panic, the circling of thoughts until they swirl in a downward spiral, that night-time self-induced frenzy, is something many of us have felt. Konstantin Levin is a very serious person, and Tolstoy gives him many of his own experiences, including the proposal scene when he and Kitty become betrothed (in a virtually wordless way). This fear of death, which will be the center of the novella *The Death of Ivan Ilych* some years later, enters Levin's consciousness as a kind of darkness. Here he manages to pull himself out of it: no matter that death will come, he needs to live while he can and accomplish some things.

In Part V of the novel this theme returns as Nikolai takes a turn for the worse. Tolstoy again narrates primarily from Kostya's point of view—he emphasizes Kostya's sensory experiences while in the sickroom, his perceptions of odor, sweat, filth, the sound of Nikolai's rasping breath, the clamminess of his skeletal hand as he grabs for his brother. Kostya is filled with disgust, and at the same time he is disgusted with himself. Always afraid of death, Kostya becomes even more fearful in its presence, until he exhausts himself to the point of indifference. We as readers perhaps judge him for thinking primarily of himself, of his own incomprehension in the face of death, but we also know that fear is but one facet of grief. Kostya's internal struggles read true to us, and his physical experience of the entire process is rendered by Tolstoy's technique of embodiment. "Levin could not look calmly at his brother, could not be natural and calm in his presence. When he entered the sick man's room, his eyes and attention would unconsciously become veiled, and he did not see or distinguish the details of his brother's condition."

In contrast, the newly married Kitty—whom Levin has not wanted to bring to his brother's deathbed—knows exactly how to improve the patient's surroundings, clean him up and make his last days more tolerable. The narrator tells us that "She had in her that excitement and quickness of judgement that appear in men before a battle, a struggle, in dangerous and decisive moments in life." According to Tolstoy, this young, inexperienced woman is capable of nursing with love and compassion. What she does is "not instinctive, animal, unreasoning," but rather correct, as if "she knew" what to do. And as Nikolai succumbs to death, Kitty is already pregnant. We might contrast Kitty's competence here with her fears and envy when, as a young, unmarried girl, she could not imagine having the bedside manner of the young woman she meets at the spa in Germany, Varenka, who is able to care for invalids selflessly and dutifully. But now we see that the mature, married Kitty has changed and she knows—wordlessly—how to alleviate Nikolai's discomfort.

The inflection points in a biography do not necessarily come quickly in Tolstoy. Instead, he draws them out, demonstrating how they affect those who are dying and those who are watching and waiting. But he also connects them, as he does with Nikolai's death and Kitty's pregnancy. And just as Tolstoy kept Nikolai alive for more than ten days, forcing Kostya and Kitty to attend him, so too he leaves Levin waiting for weeks in Moscow as the pregnant Kitty's due date comes and goes, and he finally places Levin near Kitty's side for the duration of her twenty-two-hour labor. The link between death and birth is emphasized as Levin again fails to comprehend what is happening; "he knew and felt only that what was being accomplished was similar to what had been accomplished a year ago in a hotel in a provincial capital, on the deathbed of his brother Nikolai." (Tolstoy does really write "a year earlier," rather than "last year," which would have made more sense in terms of the timing of the pregnancy. But the tension of the moment is enough that the reader only notices Kitty's extraordinarily long pregnancy, or Tolstoy's poor math skills, when we pull out the quotes!)

Levin sees this joy—and that grief—as "equally outside all ordinary circumstances of life, ... like holes in this ordinary life, through which something higher showed." In this sentence we watch Tolstoy construct those "vaults" of his narrative, and we are also brought to understand the repetition of life, of death, of sensation, in part through the repetition of individual words that describe it. In a smart comparison of two recent translations of *Anna Karenina*, Masha Gessen comments that "Tolstoy's writing is indeed remarkable for its purposeful roughness, the use of repetition and the obsessive breaking of clichés to force the reader to consider the meaning of each word and phrase." We come to Tolstoy for the moral weight, but it is the repetition that helps us feel his descriptions as *true*. The "ordinary circumstances of life" allow time to pass normally, allow us to think and function and accomplish things. But these moments of intense engagement with being, with the arrival and passing of physical bodies into and out of this world, are precisely "holes" in that ordinary timescape, and Tolstoy does his best to force us to step out of time ourselves while we are waiting for birth ... or death.

In the midst of this same chapter Levin goes for the doctor, and he is driven out of his mind that the doctor will not rush, insists on dressing, combing his hair, taking his coffee. While waiting, he finds that three minutes seem like an hour, and when the doctor brings up potential unrelated topics of conversation, Levin has to flee back to his wife's side. For the doctor, birth is a normal circumstance, even more ordinary than it is for the couple experiencing it. This scene, during which Kitty suffers and endures, and Levin begins to hate the child that will not arrive and that is causing such pain to his beloved wife, gives us a very internal look at how a husband experiences the process of birth. Having given birth myself, I'm a bit impatient with Levin's suffering which seems exaggerated, unnecessary, and unhelpful to the process, but I can appreciate that he too (and presumably Tolstoy during one or more of his wife's many childbirths) suffers, steps outside of ordinary time, and loses all sense of why this is happening at all.

Communication Strategies

For many readers, the novel *Anna Karenina* is about a failed marriage, about infidelity and the Russian social structure that does not permit the heroine of the title a second chance at happiness. We look back to that first line about happy and unhappy families and substitute the word "marriage": Tolstoy, himself notably happy in his marriage in the early years but hugely frustrated with his wife Sonya in later years (perhaps not as frustrated as she was with him!), shows us changing customs of choosing a mate, couples who communicate well or not at all, husbands and wives who don't know how to remain children of their own parents, or to become parents to their children. Marriage as a relationship is presented throughout the novel in many iterations, none of them entirely successful.

One of the most poignant moments in the book features two peripheral characters, Kostya's half-brother Sergei and the Varenka mentioned earlier. Sergei is a serious man, a philosopher, focused on government reform and the obligations of the citizen, a confirmed bachelor who had been in love as a young man with a girl who died and had not entered into new emotional engagements. Varenka, the character Kitty so admired and tried to emulate when staying at the spa in Germany, is referred to by the diminutive form of Varvara to suggest that she will forever be condescended to, looked down upon, used but not respected. Tolstoy's narrator is merciless to Varenka when she is introduced: she has a "sickly complexion," she is "a marvelous flower still full of petals, but already without color or scent." She represents a kind of death in life, a young woman left on the shelf due to financial and perhaps other circumstances. Once Kitty and Kostya have realized how happy they are in marriage, they cast about to see how they might play matchmaker. They recall Varenka and decide to see whether they can match her with the half-brother, to help bring that flower into real bloom.

In Part VI, chapters four and five, Sergei Ivanovich considers seriously whether to ask her to marry him. A group has gone mushroom hunting, and the forest feels like a wonderful setting for a proposal. Tolstoy again takes us into both head and body of the character who is preparing to act: "His heart pounded joyfully. A feeling of tenderness gripped him. He felt he had made up his mind." Varenka also expects that something is about to happen. But these two—both of whom feel that they are in love, that finally they have found a mate—will not become a couple. Instead of proposing marriage, Sergei asks a question about mushrooms, and Varenka answers. At that point, "Both he and she realized that it was over, that what ought to have been said would not be said, and their agitation, which before this had reached the highest degree, began to subside." A marriage—logical, rational, and dearly desired by both Sergei's brother Kostya and Varenka's friend Kitty—will not ensue. The awkward moment in the forest prevents this change for the two characters who in the end are doomed to remain single.

Communication is about words, the right words spoken at the right time, and it is about pacing and timing. In *Anna Karenina* it is also sometimes about wordlessness. Tolstoy narrates the experiences of the characters he has created with a certain empathy, but he does not avoid the cruelties of happenstance and circumstance. Tolstoy would argue that the best communicators do so without words, and he loves to show how the mutual understanding, and the misunderstandings, among his characters are as much about their physical actions and interactions as about the words they speak. By taking us through what I've called the inflection points of life—birth, infatuation, marriage, illness, death, though not necessarily in that order and not in one person, as would be expected in a true biography—Tolstoy constructs the vaults of his novel, connecting two (or more) worlds, two (or more) families, and leaving us with measures of joy and tragedy, not necessarily equally, as perhaps we are bound to experience in our own lives.

Love, Marriage, Sure, but a Lesson in Economics?

In *Anna Karenina*, the *bon vivant* Stiva Oblonsky—Anna's brother in Moscow—lives slightly beyond his means. His money management skills are not what they might be. When he needs to sell off the timber in a forest belonging to his wife to raise some capital, he talks about the coming deal with his friend. Konstantin Levin asks: "Did you count the trees?" Oblonsky is amused: "How can I count the trees?" And Levin answers with all the acumen of a contemporary businessman:

> No merchant will buy without counting, unless it's given away to him, as you're doing. I know your wood. I go hunting there every year, and your wood is worth two hundred rubles an acre outright, and he's given you seventy-five in installments. That means you've made him a gift of thirty thousand. … He wouldn't touch a deal where he'd make ten or fifteen percent, he waits till he gets a ruble for twenty kopeks.

Stiva doesn't want to make the effort required to establish the value of his property and instead takes the dealer's word for it. More importantly, he wants the whole business to go off in a pleasant manner and is willing to lose monetarily for the convenience of getting his result without unseemly haggling. When it leaves a bad taste in his mouth because Levin points out that he's being duped, all he wants to do is smooth things over again. And for us readers? We recognize that Stiva is careless, a frivolous man who prioritizes the immediate over what is fair and proper. We find ourselves siding with Levin, even as we recognize that his manners are rough and that his disdain for the merchant and for his friend marks him as a pedant and a grouch.

In Tolstoy we find aesthetic pleasure and moral righteousness. We find politics, farming, and good business strategies. We witness biology, and we study his ideas about communication. Reading carefully, and returning to reread, we recognize that the world is not black and white, that indeed multiple things can be true at the same time. And we learn to see not just the forest, but also the trees.

CHAPTER 4
DOSTOEVSKY, AMATEUR
PSYCHOLOGIST

Fyodor Dostoevsky (1821–1881) wrote almost a hundred years before the first edition of the American Psychiatric Association's *Diagnostic and Statistical Manual* was published in 1952. In lieu of a scientific handbook or a medical education, the author drew on his own experiences and those of acquaintances to create the inner workings of his many characters' minds. Desperation, poverty, fear, persecution, frustrated ambition and even straight-up rage—these are the emotions his characters experience, the conditions in which they find themselves, and Dostoevsky experienced many if not all of those states himself. His biography includes an arrest in 1849 for conspiring against the tsarist government to distribute banned literature. Convicted, he was exiled to Siberia and lived there among criminals and political prisoners for almost a decade—but not before famously enduring a mock execution in St. Petersburg.

I share the mock execution story with my students, who know from the course syllabus that Dostoevsky went on to write great novels, so the near-death comes as a surprise. Careful to relate the story with just the right amount of dramatic tension, I then make it clear that the faked execution was only the beginning of Dostoevsky's difficulties. Exile, severe health problems, financial disaster, family troubles, and addiction made the author miserable, but these life events also increased his empathy for the poor and the oppressed, the unfairly accused and the inherently hopeless. If his life was full of trials—in both literal and figurative senses—his books offer us ideas about how to cope with what comes down the pike. When we read Dostoevsky, we examine well-constructed characters to see what makes them tick and what drives them to violent and self-destructive, or sometimes kind and empathetic, acts. Observing them, we take lessons about how to act in our own daily lives.

We might consider Dostoevsky's novels to be carefully compiled case studies, perhaps not so much in the realm of clinical medicine as proto-clinical psychology. We would not be the first to train our eyes on the personalities he created. When psychoanalyst Sigmund Freud (1856–1939) was asked to write an article about the novel *Brothers Karamazov*, he looked at that novel, but what he really did was to analyze the novelist himself. "Dostoevsky and Parricide" (1928) offers this insight: "Four facets may be distinguished in the rich personality of Dostoevsky: the creative artist, the neurotic, the moralist and the sinner." In his essay Freud went on to locate Dostoevsky's problems in his childhood, which sounds like classic psychoanalysis. Even without analysis, Dostoevsky was fascinated with the idea that people contain within themselves conflicting desires, emotions, and even personalities. Consigning his characters to extreme situations and experiences, he brings us with him as he delves into the human psyche.

Dostoevsky loves to reveal to the reader the surprising things his characters say or do. His novels and stories are page-turners, with a broad international audience. A global stereotype of Russians is that they are more passionate, more violent, more unstable than people of some other lands. (I ran a conference once called "Those Crazy Russians" and no one got the joke.) The richest source of mad characters and neurological disorders in Russian literature, and perhaps in world literature, is Dostoevsky, with his compulsive personality, his epilepsy, and his intimate knowledge of the lives of the desperate and the downtrodden. His fiction offers a broad cast of characters whose extremes seem really extreme. At the same time events in the novels read like the front page of many a daily newspaper. *Crime and Punishment, The Idiot, The Devils, The Brothers Karamazov*: published over the course of only about fifteen years, Dostoevsky's four "great novels" feature impoverished students, political intrigue, society misfortunes, and the overheated life of a northern Russian town. They give us insight into different levels of society and particularly into the lives of young people. For example, one of the most compelling characters in *The Brothers Karamazov*, the youngest brother Alyosha Karamazov, is painfully truthful and simultaneously self-absorbed, filled with the self-doubt but also the bravery and honesty that are the hallmarks of adolescence in full force.

We can read these novels when we are safely on the other side of adolescence, gaining insights into our own lives and those of our children, our students, our neighbors. However, I maintain that since Dostoevsky's fiction represents the adolescent mindset and experiences particularly well—he even has a novel entitled *The Raw Youth*—I would argue that it speaks directly to (and about) the adolescent or young adult reader.

In lectures I quote an odd fact I dug up in my archival research almost twenty years ago. In 1905, at the Kiev Second Congress of Psychiatrists, the doctors gathered felt the need to take a stand against tsarist-era judicial practices of capital punishment. To emphasize their point, they proclaimed:

> Capital punishment deprives of life and a future those who have not yet shown what they can contribute to society. Indeed, had the sentence been carried out, the tsarist government would have executed our beloved progenitor, Fyodor Dostoevsky, who faced a firing squad for illegal behavior in 1849. Where would Russian psychiatry be today without the examples of mental illness sprinkled throughout Dostoevsky's novels?

Psychiatrists in Russia saw Dostoevsky's literary efforts as a proto-textbook. Because long before Russia had a class of professionals who tried to diagnose and treat mental illness, Dostoevsky was exploring the human mind, with its contradictions, perversions, and willfulness. Psychiatrists, psychologists, and sociologists the world over continue to admire Dostoevsky. As did Freud, a topic to which we will return.

So do readers, adolescent ones in particular. Isn't that the age when it seems most critical to come down on one side or the other of debates about capital punishment? In the United States, disaffected young men see themselves in the angry protagonist of *Notes from Underground* ("I am just like that character!" one declared to a friend of mine during a suburban Detroit high-school graduation party back in the mid-1980s). I have had students come to class, diagnostic manual in hand, wanting to clarify why the main character of Dostoevsky's popular novel *Crime and Punishment*, Rodion Raskolnikov, did what he did. Usually, the diagnosis comes back as antisocial personality disorder.

Dostoevsky is a master of psychological trauma. Throughout his narratives we find different kinds of trauma and trauma-inducing actions: imposter syndrome, drunkenness and addictive behavior, self-sabotage, and the *Doppelgänger* phenomenon to name just a few. Dostoevsky's style of narration frequently brings us into the heads of his characters, so that we experience their psychological states along with them—often suddenly. In *Crime and Punishment*, for instance, Dostoevsky uses the word *vdrug* (which means *suddenly*) to mark a shift in the action or an abrupt psychological change five hundred and sixty times. In fact, he used that word over five thousand times in his entire written corpus—it was one of his favorites.

This and other types of rapid shifts in the novel are of course part of a marketing style. His novels were serialized in monthly magazines and needed to maintain a certain urgency to keep the reader engaged. But *vdrug* also implies a discomfort with the world, a kind of obstinacy, even obstreperousness, that might mark a character with another DSM diagnosis—oppositional personality disorder.

And that opposition is real. In many of his novels Dostoevsky places a version of the Russian cultural figure of the "holy fool" on a collision course with society—that too is a familiar type from most high-school classrooms, the guy (usually) who insists on playing the class clown or on not conforming to societal expectations regardless of social pressures. Dostoevsky's attention to psychological detail makes these characters and others rise off the page and seem to interact with his readers. We recognize them as human beings, and sometimes we recognize ourselves in them. Psychologists have shown that when readers identify with fictional characters it lights up the same part of the brain as when they think about themselves. This is one of the ways in which novels take us on journeys as we read—it's like a buddy movie, just with the invented character and our own psyche together in the front seat of a vehicle. The experience of reading such novels also reminds us of what it meant to be a self-focused adolescent trying to sort out our identity.

We can look to Dostoevsky's protagonists from across his entire body of work to find case studies for various mental conditions—schizophrenics or alcoholics, big bear-like men raging with anger or skinny meek ones suffering from martyr complexes, sexual predators or unreasonable optimists, mental midgets or megalomaniacs, women in the grips of hysteria or high on their power over others. I believe these characters tell us more about the human condition than "normal" people ever will, despite their marriages and infidelities and protracted births or lingering illnesses leading to death. Tolstoy's world was larger than life, and in Dostoevsky, the characters are.

The Double

In *Crime and Punishment*, my students identify doubles and foils of the main hero in virtually every character and explain how Raskolnikov's many perceived doubles each takes a path he too might choose, might have chosen. This novel becomes a schematized web of connected people, all of whom function as Raskolnikov's potential doubles. In our own lives, we frequently hear about or see a person who looks just like us. That sense that we have a *Doppelgänger* wandering the world, reacting as we do or indeed making the opposite choices, is more than a fictional trope. But as fictional tropes go, it is one of the best. Mary Shelley's *Frankenstein* (1818), Edgar Allan Poe's *William Wilson* (1839), Robert Louis Stevenson's *Dr. Jekyll and Mr. Hyde* (1886), Oscar Wilde's *Dorian Gray* (1890): each character pair in these literary works has its own contribution to make to the literature of the queer, the unsettling, the Gothic. The literature of *Doppelgängers*.

In fiction from across the Russian empire, we also find a lot of doubles. Nikolai Gogol puts forward the neighbors Ivan Ivanovich and Ivan Nikiforovich in his story "How Ivan Ivanovich Argued with Ivan Nikiforovich" (1835), and he counts on the comic relief generated by his twin-like Pyotr Ivanovich Bobchinsky and Pyotr Ivanovich

Dobchinsky in his 1836 play *The Inspector General*. As we will see later, Dostoevsky also indulges in this literary structure, producing somewhat ridiculous creatures. In the twentieth century Vladimir Nabokov lampoons Dostoevsky in *Despair* (1937), a crime novel in which the murderer tries to frame a person he believes to be his double but who actually looks nothing like him at all. A mistake like that really could lead to despair! This is only one example of the many doubled characters in Nabokov's novels.

The very idea of the double, that there is someone out there just like us, should be comforting, particularly for adolescents who feel so alone, so certain that their experiences are unique, that they suffer as no one has before or since. Instead, it makes us uncomfortable. To push the uncanny aside, to protect ourselves from that which we fear, we often use foreign language terms in English (such as *Doppelgänger*, *déjà vu*). Dostoevsky brought those concepts into his fiction to make us confront our psychological problems.

The young Dostoevsky made his debut with the 1845 epistolary novel *Poor Folk* that told the tale of a humble and proud man named Makar Devushkin. Makar suffers from his poverty and the low nature of his position. Seeing that not everyone shares his fate, he entertains dreams of potential love and happiness, dreams that turn out to be mere delusions. In imagining a future, he dares to think "why shouldn't I be happy?" and subsequently is dealt a crushing blow. A mature man in his fifties, his anxieties resemble those of an adolescent, and he experiences the same desires to change his station and find his happiness as will torture Raskolnikov.

That pride lies at the core of many of Dostoevsky's novels, and it's one of the things that appeals to readers. In *Crime and Punishment*, we can talk about the pride of the poor and how ambition, or even the desire to live a life like others, a happy, even prosperous life, can drive people to the brink. When Makar Devushkin doesn't fit in, doesn't seem to rate, we wonder about society's expectations and feel for the character who cannot meet them. Dostoevsky's clerk in his second novella *The Double* (1846), Golyadkin, is bedeviled by a second Golyadkin who seems to have usurped him. Like Devushkin, Golyadkin has contradictory dreams, dreams that foresee the young

Raskolnikov's frustrations: Golyadkin wants to be like everyone else, but at the same time be an independent operator.

These two desires, to fit in and to stand out, to be "normal" and yet extraordinary, to be protected from seeming ridiculous or from getting hurt while also becoming an autonomous agent who can and does make his own decisions, lead Golyadkin down the path of paranoia and separate him from the "reality" in which he lives. He suffers from an existential loneliness that causes him to become confused, fills him with a terrifying anguish, and forces a disintegration of his personality. In this early work Dostoevsky borrowed the idea of doubling from E. T. A. Hoffmann and from Nikolai Gogol, who believed that people should stay in their own place, should not dream or reach for a station above the one they occupy. Dostoevsky's spin on the plot led to him being grouped with Gogol and even with Pushkin (who gave us a mad Eugene in his 1833 Petersburg poem *The Bronze Horseman*), as writers who showed empathy for the "little man" caught in the wheels of the bureaucratic imperial city. In *Crime and Punishment* Dostoevsky developed that existential personality conflict further.

For readers today, that conflict is familiar from developmental psychology textbooks and more intimately from our own adolescent lives. And perhaps we condemn the delusional Devushkin, Golyadkin, and Raskolnikov. It is familiar, though. We have had these thoughts or know someone who has: If everything breaks my way, if this lottery ticket turns out to be a winner, if I get that promotion, I'll have what it takes to become a hero—to buy the fast cars, take the fancy vacations, score the handsome guy.

Knowing the difference between fact and fiction, between what is possible and what is portrayed for us on the page and more especially these days on the screen (and in social media), we live our non-heroic lives. But that takes time to learn, to comprehend that the house always wins, that those fantasy couples on television or Instagram really are too beautiful to be real. In fiction we can watch the ambition of others run amok. The idea that it is safer not to dream fantastic dreams, to keep our personalities and ambitions in check, to agree to seek out other measures of success that do not map onto the ambitious and heroic, qualifies as a "grown up" judgment that can lead to a small but stable life. However, that way of approaching our interactions with the world is more than a little depressing. That's part of what Dostoevsky offers us: a view into characters who keep dreaming despite their failures and frustrations. In a way, he offers us hope.

Dostoevsky's texts are driven by these remarkable characters, and his skill in constructing the worlds in which they live brings the smells and sounds of those worlds to his readers. It is in *Crime and Punishment* that the anxieties of adolescence emerge most vividly, and they make even murder feel almost normal in Dostoevsky's St. Petersburg. Let's take a stroll with Rodion Raskolnikov along the streets of the imperial capital and explore with Dostoevsky his young character's existential loneliness.

The Loner and the Crowd

The novel *Crime and Punishment* opens on a hot and sultry day in the city. The oppressive air restricts the readers' breathing too as we follow a young man who is planning and then rapidly commits a violent double murder. Not much more than fifty pages in, two women are dead, laying in pools of their own blood. This is no *whodunit*—we know that Raskolnikov has plotted and planned this act, and we watch as it goes horribly wrong. But even though we spend time with him, walking the streets, listening to him mutter to himself, watching him toss and turn in his little "coffin" of an attic room as he tortures himself both before and after the murders, we never quite know *why* he did it. One answer—that comes to the reader of Dostoevsky's other fiction—lies in the existential personality conflict of the lonely, ambitious man.

Recently I've been proposing to students that in seeking to understand the reasons for the crime, and some of the pressure on the young Raskolnikov, we should consider the many other characters who crowd their way into the first two parts of the novel, and in particular two who finally appear a third of a way into the novel, on the last two pages of Part II: Raskolnikov's mother Pulkheria Alexandrovna and his sister Dunya.

What surprises readers most when they begin to read this novel is not the crime—that they saw coming, given the title—but the sheer number of people present in the opening pages. The text teems with names just as the crowded city teems with people: Raskolnikov, Alyona Ivanovna, Lizaveta, Nastasya, Praskovya Pavlovna, but also Marmeladov, Katerina Ivanovna and her three little children (Polechka, Kolya, and Lidochka, still unnamed at this point), Amalia Fyodorovna, Darya Frantsevna, Lebezyatnikov, Klopstock Ivan Ivanovich (who is only named because he failed to pay for the shirts he ordered), Kapernaumov and his wife and children, and of course Sonechka Marmeladova. Some of them appear in the flesh in the pages of Part I, while others are merely evoked. By the end of Part II this multitude of characters has become more than just names; most have actually shown up in the narrative; others will shortly.

One particularly vital group of people for the novel's plot and for understanding Raskolnikov's state of mind appears thanks to an inserted text. In Part I, Chapter 3 Raskolnikov receives a letter from his mother, who introduces a whole slew of new names from her provincial life: Svidrigailov, Marfa Petrovna, Pyotr Petrovich Luzhin, Afanasy Ivanovich Vakhrushin. The letter is a preposterous proposition in itself—and a nightmare for a young man who is trying to sort out his feelings and aspirations while away at school. You may be far from home, but your mom can always lecture you.

Though the letter is supposedly just two pages long, the words are representative of the crowds in a St. Petersburg square: it seems impossible that so much text could fit onto two pieces of paper. This breach of "reality" in a realist novel highlights the importance of the letter. Through it two characters—Raskolnikov's closest kin, his mother Pulkheria Alexandrovna and his beloved sister Dunya—enter the narrative and begin to live in the reader's imagination long before they actually appear in his St. Petersburg garret.

In the chapter following the inserted letter, Raskolnikov argues aloud with his mother and sister despite the fact that they are nowhere to be seen. This conversation, provoked by the epistolary haranguing of Pulkheria Alexandrovna, fixes these two women as essential characters in Part I of the novel and, one could even argue, figures them as active catalysts to the murder of the other two women. As Raskolnikov thinks through how society is constructed, and what role a young provincial man might play in it, he decides that he should seize the power he lacks. Asserting that he wants to test his will, he implements his plan to kill Alyona Ivanovna, the pawnbroker whom he has identified as a socially harmful "louse" sucking the blood of the impoverished.

Even fictional people must take responsibility for their actions, and there is no doubt who is to blame for the murders Raskolnikov commits. Nonetheless Raskolnikov's family, present in his head at the moment of his heightened isolation, and his sense of obligation toward them are a second indirect cause of the deaths of Alyona Ivanovna and her sister Lizaveta. Two deaths don't make Raskolnikov a serial killer, but his psychological profile can spring to mind now when we see young (usually) men in the United States and elsewhere who turn weapons on innocent people. Lizaveta, at any rate, was completely innocent. Her death evokes those tragic deaths that happen in real life and choke our newsfeeds in today's world. Crowded, and endlessly sad.

In these first two parts of the novel, the contrast between Raskolnikov's loneliness and perpetual aloneness and the people (and ideas) in his head with whom he constantly converses and argues paints Raskolnikov as a loner in a crowd. His visit to Dmitry Razumikhin in Part II, Chapter 2 strengthens this sense. Having come seeking assistance, Raskolnikov lashes out at his friend: "But now I see that I don't want anything, do you hear, anything at all … I want nobody's help or pity … I myself … alone … Oh, that's enough! Leave me in peace. Leave me in peace." Raskolnikov has come to Razumikhin, and at this point they are alone in the latter's apartment. Moments later he silently rejects the translation work Razumikhin has offered him to help him earn some much-needed cash. This reaching out for help, and then angrily rejecting that assistance, is the dilemma of the adolescent. He wants to be independent, to manage on his own, and when he cannot, his pride prevents him from taking freely given aid, even from a friend.

Although the narration does not at this juncture show readers what is going on inside Raskolnikov's head, we have the sense that he has been made deaf by the many voices careening around up there: stumbling back out of Razumikhin's building, Raskolnikov does not notice the crowded street or the cries of a cabby, and as a result he is almost run over by a horse-drawn cab. A loner in a crowd, he is brought back to sensation by physical contact.

Here we might pause a moment to recall Dostoevsky himself and certainly the dissatisfied characters from those first two pieces of fiction, *Poor Folk* and *The Double*, both of which he published before his arrest, trial, and exile to Siberia in 1849. "I myself ... alone." These are the words of a young person trying to become independent, trying to make his way in the world, and failing miserably. At that age it is particularly hard to turn to others for help, to depend on a support system, when all you want is to grow up already and live an autonomous life. Himself still in his twenties at the time, Dostoevsky created powerless male characters in these first two novellas who retain that adolescent resentment, though he makes them old enough to know better, with Golyadkin in *The Double* in his forties and Makar Devushkin of *Poor Folk* in his fifties. Unfulfilled ambition keeps them bitter, angry, impotent, and alone.

In Raskolnikov, Dostoevsky returns to the promising young man. The character's frustrations are exacerbated by the expectations that accompanied him on his move to the capital to study law. His provincial family believes in his intelligence, his capacity to negotiate the university and the city, and what they see as his inevitable future achievements—fame, fortune, stability, the ability to make his family proud. As he retreats from his friend Razumikhin's apartment in haste, Raskolnikov is very far from reaching or even wanting these goals.

Feeling the lash of the whip and the alms pressed into his palm by concerned passersby—two physical gestures made by human beings who actually touch his body—the murderer suddenly becomes aware of just how isolated he is. In Part I of the novel, he actually carried out his plan, and in Part II Raskolnikov becomes even more desperate than before. His cognitive choice to not take Razumikhin's help, followed by this instinctive rejection of human pity when he throws the money into the river, underline Raskolnikov's new status as eternal loner. Crowd or no crowd, he cannot sustain contact with other human beings. As the narrator puts it, "he felt that he had in that moment cut himself [off] from everybody and everything, as with a knife."

However, as with much in this rapidly moving novel, this is not entirely true: just a few chapters later (Part II, Chapter 7), when the drunken Marmeladov actually does fall beneath the wheels of a cab, Raskolnikov goes out of his way to help the dying man's family. Even this effort, seemingly antithetical to Raskolnikov's idea that he has "cut himself off," highlights the psychological and physical isolation that was arguably one of the primary reasons for his criminal act in the first place. His promises to the widow ("I … in short, I will come again") and his entreaties to Marmeladov's stepdaughter Polechka to pray for him are not the cause of his sudden pride and self-confidence; instead, they represent a pull toward human contact that is just as rapidly followed by a desire to be alone, as it had been earlier: "I myself." I can stand on my own. Though impoverished, Raskolnikov is drawn to help and then just as quickly remembers his own powerless status, now made worse by having committed the pointless murders.

This question, of whether we want to live our lives embedded in a web of social connections or whether we long to strike out on our own, live by our wits and talents, is one that tortures us all in our early adult years. The anxieties of adolescence. It's hard to avoid them. Raskolnikov—who has been named by his creator Dostoevsky after the very concept of the "split personality," since the Russian word *raskol* refers to a split—was pushed onto the road of ambition with a little help from his family. He is kind … and cruel. He is thoughtful … and viciously selfish. Rodion Raskolnikov is throughout the novel poised on the knife's edge between these two states, and his actions contradict each other as though there were two of him, as though he were a double in one body, his own personal *Doppelgänger*.

The arrival of the letter from his mother at such an important juncture in Raskolnikov's planning of the crime may be seen as critical to its perpetration. Pulled out of his own head, out of his aloneness, into the lives of his family, including being told at length in the letter of their trials, tribulations, and even suffering on his behalf, Raskolnikov enters into an imagined argument with these dear creatures. They populate his consciousness, and he engages them as vociferously and intensely as he has the rational utilitarian arguments for and against murder over the past month, lying on his couch. We might even accuse Raskolnikov's mother and sister of moving the murders from "dream" to reality. And that is the real adolescent dream: You take action, even making significant, fatal errors, but it's not really your fault. You can blame it on your mother.

Russian Reactions and Russian Reality

It was over a hundred fifty years ago that Dostoevsky started publishing his novel *Crime and Punishment* in installments in the Moscow journal the *Russian Herald*. The novel appeared monthly over the course of 1866, and it was a smash hit. As one influential critic put it at the time: "During the year 1866 only *Crime and Punishment* was being read, only it was being spoken about by fans of literature, who often complained about the stifling power of the novel and the painful impression it left which caused people with strong nerves to risk illness and forced those with weak nerves to give up reading it altogether."

We know why we read the novel—to explore the mind of a young man in extremis, to understand what could drive a person to think he has the power of life and death over others. But what caused this novel to take Russia by storm in the nineteenth century?

At the time, Russian society was struck by the boldness of Dostoevsky's idea. For some critics, the murders of pawnbroker Alyona Ivanovna and her sister Lizaveta, committed by ex-student Rodion Raskolnikov, were "the purest absurdity." But others immediately began to see coincidence with current events. After all, on January 12, 1866, just days after the first instalment of *Crime and Punishment* was published, a student by the name of Danilov committed a similar crime: killing a moneylender and his servant and robbing their apartment. In the wake of this event, Dostoevsky's detailed description of how the violent crime was planned seemed prescient. Literary critic Nikolai Strakhov maintained that the public supposed Danilov's crime to be related to "the general nihilistic conviction that all means were permitted to improve an unreasonable state of affairs," a conviction shared by Dostoevsky's protagonist Raskolnikov.

It's worth defining that "unreasonable state of affairs" in tsarist Russia. Among other things, young Russian radicals believed that in the wake of the emancipation of the serfs in 1861, the peasantry should have risen up against the autocracy. Imagining that the Russian people might embody the socialist principles radicals espoused, some radicals expected further social changes and dreamed of a humanitarian society that would arise to replace the status quo. Other radicals thought that the answer to Russian woes was the development of capitalism and further industrialization, led by enlightened members of the intelligentsia in the direction of economic (and social) progress for all. Such multiple divisions in society—conservatives versus radicals, but then the radicals among themselves—feel familiar today in many parts of the world. At the time, the Russian government panicked and tried to suppress public discussions of these issues.

Some of these radical youth called themselves "nihilists" and preached a need to overturn society. Though the aim of many of their ideas was altruistic and humanitarian—a desire to alleviate human suffering and to distribute wealth and opportunities among a larger swath of the population—their methods were sometimes violent. And the results were clearly on display on April 4, 1866, when a young student named Dmitry Karakozov took a shot at Tsar Alexander II.

Dostoevsky himself was shocked and horrified at this turn of events—midway through the writing and publication of his tremendously successful novel—almost as much by his fear of government reprisals as by his disbelief that a Russian would raise his hand against the autocrat. Dostoevsky intended the novel more than anything to be about human happiness, certainly not as a fictional take on current events. As he wrote in his notebook: "man is not born for happiness. Man earns his happiness, and always by suffering," which for him corresponded to the definition of Orthodox Christianity. In the novel readers watch as the central character, a lapsed Christian, commits a crime, suffers for having done it, and then is redeemed and given the chance for happiness through that very suffering. Dostoevsky had not intended to write a topical novel about the student Danilov, nor to give ideas to Karakozov and thereby endanger the life of the tsar. He intended to move a young man onto a path to redemption.

Raskolnikov's misdeeds are as much against god and man as they are against society and the law, which is one reason the novel remains a staple for young readers. The age of the young radical was essential for Dostoevsky's conception of his protagonist too. As he jotted to himself in his notebook: "In writing [the novel], do not forget that he is 23 years old."

If *Crime and Punishment* is not a *whodunit* it is certainly a thriller. The plot centers around a young man who is frustrated with the social and financial opportunities available to him, a young man who believes he can and should seize his own destiny. Written by a self-made man whose own life up to this point had been full of trauma, the novel offers a path to redemption for both the criminal and the sinner. For Dostoevsky himself, certainly, if not for terrorist Dmitry Karakozov.

With the historical events of 1866 in faraway Russia now long forgotten by most readers, *Crime and Punishment* stands as a novel of ideas, in which philosophies of life are incarnated in various characters. The novel interrogates the right of man to violate social norms and conventions and to choose his own path in life regardless of his social status. For Dostoevsky, it was a "psychological account of a crime." But for Russians one hundred and fifty plus years ago, it felt almost like journalism—an account of an unhinged student who commits acts of terrorism.

Radical Personalities

When I lecture on Dostoevsky, I tend to focus on those four "great novels" (*Crime and Punishment, The Idiot, The Devils* and *The Brothers Karamazov*). These major works include a wide spectrum of humanity operating in dramatic historical times. *The Idiot* takes as its title a character with diminished—or perhaps divine—personality traits, a man who is mild and good. His name, Prince Myshkin, signals to Russian readers that he is as gentle as a mouse (*mysh'* in Russian).

Those who know Russian medieval history recognize in him the "holy fool," but Dostoevsky here offers a new take on that cultural trope. Myshkin emerges from a medically sheltered life naïve and curious and by the end of the novel retreats back to that shelter, perhaps further traumatized by the human actions and emotions of murder, anger and revenge that he experiences in the world. *The Devils*, one of my favorites, dissects a nihilist cell in another provincial town, examining the roles played by various members and other people in the community and indicting the dangerous games played by political extremists. We only have time in a semester to read one novel, so I usually go with *Crime and Punishment* and add the shorter *Notes from Underground* (1864) as feasible.

Dostoevsky's last novel was *The Brothers Karamazov*: his longest and grandest novel. Here he launches a new experiment into human psychology, one that perhaps still is not included in the DSM. The novelist gives us four brothers, each the occupant of an extreme quadrant of the human psyche, the union of which might have made a reasonable psychological whole. Each, reacting to their father and to other figures of authority, behaves, I'm afraid I have to say it, like an adolescent boy. The novel again features a murder, though this time we don't actually know who committed it. Any of the four main characters might have killed the evil patriarch Fyodor Karamazov, and good riddance to him. It turns out (not much of a spoiler) that his three legitimate sons from two wives—Ivan the intellectual, Dmitry the passionate impulsive one, and Alexei or Alyosha the mild, kind, religious one—have another half-brother, the result of Fyodor's rape of a local mentally deficient woman known as the half-wit Stinking Lizaveta. Smerdyakov (whose surname emerges from the word for "stinking," his mother's moniker) is a cowering toady, but also somehow aggressive, and together the four brothers represent extreme versions of different personality types. In one person, perhaps, all the bad character traits might have cancelled each other out and created a multifaceted thoughtful and intelligent man, but in isolation none of the brothers is functional.

Remember Freud and his assessment of Dostoevsky's personality, which he saw as consisting of four facets that are poorly integrated? In many of his works, as we've discussed, Dostoevsky has doubles, pairs of characters, and foils: Raskolnikov could have taken the path down which Svidrigailov strode at the end of *Crime and Punishment*, or he could have taken himself in hand and made a game of the poverty he was experiencing, the way the passionate Dmitry Razumikhin did. He also could have used his gender, along with the good looks, superior intelligence, and moral backbone he shared with his sister Dunya, to move through the world in ways that she as a woman could not. Raskolnikov ignores all the examples around him and himself splits in two between the cold-blooded intellectually motivated murderer and the instinctive empathetic young man who helps the prostitute and pays for her father's funeral. All of those doubles, foils and split personalities make us as readers amateur psychologists too as we think about choices made and options spurned. We read in the epilogue to the novel about Raskolnikov's redemption and potential reintegration—into one human personality and into the society around him—but we may not believe in it.

In *Brothers Karamazov* Dostoevsky takes us to a new level. He doubles his fun by inventing four brothers, four characters instead of two (or just one with a split personality). The father, Fyodor Karamazov, seems himself to be on the brink of insanity. His rages and his buffoonish behavior are painful to read about, but our pain is nothing compared to the excruciating embarrassment experienced by his sons. One example: a meal at the monastery where the youngest brother, Alyosha, has been living in hopes of becoming a monk himself or at least staying as close as possible to his mentor, the holy elder Father Zossima. Alyosha's desire to step outside the secular world and immerse himself in a religious community is again recognizable from our own adolescence or that of people we know. Deprived of a normal family life by among others his scandal-mongering father, he longs for routine, for dependability. Certainly, many organized religions and even the cults young people sometimes join offer regular prayer or meditation, communal meals and ritualized self-deprivation, authority figures and authoritative texts to be followed. When later in the novel Alyosha strives to create community among a set of boys who have squabbled among themselves, teaching them by example and helping them to learn to care for one another, Dostoevsky is giving us a more positive version of the ties that can bind. If family life is rarely a haven for Dostoevsky's characters, he does recognize the need for and create opportunities for people to belong to each other. He also notes the jealousy fathers sometimes feel when their sons choose other mentors; perhaps that's why Fyodor behaves so badly at the monastery meal.

This meal is just one instance in a novel filled with drama, in a town that resembles a madhouse, *durdom* as the Russians might say. Such scenes have given rise to what has been called the Dostoevskian *nadryv*, a scandal with elements of frenzy. We would never encounter anything so extreme in our own cultures (or so we tell ourselves), and yet scenes throughout *Brothers Karamazov* and Dostoevsky's other great novels echo our everyday experiences or at least what we read in the newspaper and in social media—conversations in taverns and in market squares; inquiries at police stations, interrogations, and courtroom dramas; family dynamics marked by misunderstandings, secrets, and covert self-sacrifice. Everything has that extra measure of drama that is a hallmark of Dostoevsky's fiction, but it all feels familiar, like our own lives reflected in a funhouse mirror. Like madhouses, funhouses are never actually that fun.

It can seem to the reader that this drama represents a profound honesty, although in Dostoevsky's characters more often than not it turns out to be pure self-delusion and self-absorption. Part of the reason these characters have the time to indulge in self-absorption is because in Dostoevsky characters rarely go out to work in any serious way. Thus, the rhythms of these novels are made up of those same emotional extremes that we experience in adolescence. As we read them again upon reaching maturity, we notice that our own lives are grounded in the routines and everyday actions and activities that keep the world moving. We get up, put on a pair of pants, eat some breakfast and go out into society. With our busy lives we don't often think about who is looking at us, or how we can cheat the system to get the big windfall instead of working every day and earning our paychecks. We don't scheme to murder our fathers or to steal money from our fiancés. Certainly not as grown-ups.

And *suddenly*, as Dostoevsky might have said, events take a new turn. In Dostoevsky's fiction we plumb the depths of human nature and the human psyche, and his fellow Russian writers (and readers of all kinds) honor that in him, seeing in him a proto-psychologist. In my view, and not only in mine, Dostoevsky is a great writer, influential and deep, of course, but also frenetic and even fun. That's a lot to deliver, and he does it in work after work.

CHAPTER 5
CHEKHOV AND THE PLEASURES OF
THE WRITTEN WORD

Anton Chekhov (1860–1904) famously never wrote a novel. So, writing about Chekhov, an archetypal short story writer, after delving into Tolstoy and Dostoevsky may seem counterintuitive. But as a student of mine once said toward the end of a long term, "Chekhov really fits an undergraduate's schedule." And there is something particularly lovely about the short form. Chekhov wrote countless short stories, internationally admired plays, and brilliant if sometimes didactic personal letters. In every genre, Chekhov enables us to experience the pleasure of the written word.

Part of that pleasure is in the empathy we feel with characters and their life situations, and as a consummate creator of characters, Chekhov is among the best at helping us experience the lives of those who may be very different from us. For example, a few years ago I read "Small Fry," one of Chekhov's early stories, with a group of students. When the narrator proclaimed about the unhappy protagonist that "his need for a new and better life made his heart ache with unbearable anguish," one young woman burst out: "I know just how he feels."

As witnessed by this student's response, Chekhov portrays suffering particularly well. In isolation the sentence may seem overdramatic, but it also rings true. Chekhov has a way of putting things, a way of expressing feelings, of describing places, of presenting situations that both brings aesthetic enjoyment and sometimes causes a bitter shaking of the head—yes, I know that, yes, I too have felt that. In his play *Uncle Vanya*, the plain Sonya wonders whether it is better to know the truth, or to remain hopeful in the face of what seems like obviously unrequited love. Watching Sonya suffer helps us understand our own not infrequent desire to delude ourselves and others—or perhaps it helps to comprehend the consequences of our choice not to do so.

Other works—like arguably Chekhov's most famous story, "The Lady with a Pet Dog"—evoke one reaction among twenty-somethings and an entirely different reaction at later stages of life. The December–May romance featured in the story often repels my students but feels poignant to older readers, and the story's lack of resolution makes its ending, too, seem true-to-life—if a tad unsettling. Careful readers note both reactions: even those who are grossed out by the idea of a forty-something man pursuing a girl in her twenties realize that she is eager, bored with her own life, seeking an escape from the early marriage that was such a mistake. So off-putting, but also compelling. Why does she go to him? What does she see in him?

Fascinating character portrayals aside, Chekhov's work is not only about people or plot. Within many of his stories there are aesthetic moments that transport the reader, engaging all the senses and yielding paragraphs for reading and rereading. In "Lady" too we experience those vivid sensations, and the contrast to "gray" reality, also presented in the story, becomes even more prominent. Portraying emotions convincingly takes a light hand, and painting landscapes with words is a particular talent. We read Chekhov for these pleasures and more.

The Resort Town of Yalta

When I think about Crimea now, I have three immediate impressions: my sadness that in the current political state of the world the lands there are contested and liable to see even more turmoil in the years to come. My recollections of walks, talks, and vistas I experienced when I did visit the Black Sea region several times in the 2000s. And a more general curiosity about the many people who have visited and lived in Crimea over the centuries, sometimes pursuing a livelihood but also in search of health cures, and distraction, and love. We read about spa culture in Jane Austen's rendition of life in Bath, England, but in Crimea we have mountains alongside an inland sea. Dramatic landscapes. It's a destination for sure, if for many readers only a literary one. The ancient lands and their original peoples have been overrun, claimed, fought over, deported, returned, and reframed so many times that their complex history is rarely evoked, though I have a feeling that throughout the twenty-first century Crimea will be remembered and fought over some more.

Chekhov's "Lady with a Pet Dog" was written in 1899. In the story, Chekhov uses toponyms and specific places that we can find in old caches of postcards—like Vernet's, the seaside restaurant where the protagonist meets the lady and her dog—and that other tourists have visited since, such as the bench someone placed at Oreanda, a location up the hill from Yalta itself with views in all directions. I have sat on that bench.

Even now, if you make it to Yalta, you can go and look out over the Black Sea, listening for the sounds that echo the ones Dmitry and Anna Sergeevna heard in Chekhov's story:

> In Oreanda they sat on a bench not far from the church, looked down on the sea, and were silent. Yalta was barely visible through the morning mist, white clouds stood motionless on the mountaintops. The leaves of the trees did not stir, cicadas called, and the monotonous, dull noise of the sea, coming from below, spoke of the peace, of the eternal sleep that awaits us. So it had sounded below when neither Yalta nor Oreanda were there, so it sounded now and would go on sounding with the same dull indifference when we are no longer here. And in this constancy, in this utter indifference to the life and death of each of us, there perhaps lies hidden the pledge of our eternal salvation, the unceasing movement of life on earth, of unceasing perfection.

This passage, coming as it does after the couple has met, begun to share their days, and even consummated the sexual part of their relationship, takes readers outside of themselves. It "fits" both the mood of the piece, with its tender, gay and yet sad protagonists, and the resort aspect of the setting. A spring vacation, far from the cold, harsh responsibility of their home lives, a chance to breathe the healthy sea air and to stroll in the hills, to listen to the silence and to the sounds of the sea, to get physically tired out and in so doing rest intellectually and spiritually.

The sounds of that eternal sea are themselves healing. I know—I can still hear the lapping of the waves outside the balcony window at the former Soviet health resort I stayed at when I attended a Chekhov conference in Yalta in 2008. I can still smell that very specific iodine-infused saltwater sea. But Chekhov's description—which up to now in the story has been mostly in the head of the hero Dmitry Gurov—moves into a different register here, and then just as quickly brings us back to Gurov.

> Sitting beside the young woman, who looked so beautiful in the dawn, appeased and enchanted by the view of this magical décor—sea, mountains, clouds, the open sky—Gurov reflected that, essentially, if you thought about it, everything was beautiful in this world, everything except for what we ourselves think and do when we forget the higher goals of being and our human dignity.

The setting of Yalta and the hills above it are "décor" to Gurov, a stage set for his affair with the younger woman, Anna Sergeevna. We have watched as something akin to a play unfolded: a chance meeting on the promenade, regular strolls and conversations, an intimate scene in a hotel room, and now this bird's-eye view that seems to see into the past and the future simultaneously. That last bit of text, where Gurov take us into the past and the future, is one reason this is a story and not a play. Instead of attending to a monologue pronounced from center stage, readers are *in* the text, hear the sea shushing away, sit alongside Dmitry and Anna, imagine themselves on that bench in Oreanda. Before we look more closely at the relationship, let's pause on that sound.

In Russian, the sounds in that paragraph fill the scene even when they are explicitly denied. "The leaves of the trees did not stir"—but in so doing, we hear *ne shevelilas*. The rustling *sh* sound is there though the breeze, and hence the leaves, are still. Going on: the sound of the cicadas in Russian gives us *kr, ch, ts, k*, and the sea gives us *z, kh, sh, s, sh, s, s, z*. The word "noise" or "sound" in Russian is *shum*—perhaps we should write it phonetically as *shoom*—and that sound repeats in the verb describing what the sea does, in past tense, present and future. The indifference echoes the sound, with its stressed syllable, *dush* or *doosh*, also shushing, and the "perfection" at the end of the sentence gives a stressed syllable of *shen*. For an English-language reader this soundscape does not mimic the *shushing* of the sea as closely as Chekhov's original does. But the *s* sounds are there: mist, trees, cicadas, monotonous, sea, peace, sleep. Sounded, constancy, indifference, salvation, unceasing. It is soothing, soft, indeed monotonous, but in that reassuring way the world has of reminding us that it will go on when we are no longer here. We are part of the universe and we are also utterly inconsequential. The sound orchestration delivers Chekhov's thought to readers with no trouble at all, even in translation.

The man who sees Anna Sergeevna off at the train station at the end of the story's second part brings that feeling of the sea again: in Russian Dmitry Gurov is *schastlivy*, happy or even lucky (the word means both), mostly as a consequence of his holiday at the sea and the lovely woman with whom he spent it. After all, as the narrator tells us, he is "almost twice her age" (*starshe*, again with the shushing). This is that fleeting happiness celebrated by poets and in its beauty somehow not at all banal.

For my college students, this infidelity seems wrong, exploitative, a creepy older man taking advantage of an unhappy younger woman. And in our #MeToo moment of the 2020s, that is an important context. For many others, however, the sensitivity with which Chekhov treats both his main characters makes the relationship all right. After all, their lives—each so unhappy in his or her own way and each seeking the solace of human connection at this seaside resort—speak to the rhythms of older readers' experiences.

Like Tolstoy's *Anna Karenina*, with which "Lady" is in a relationship of its own and which, of course, features lots of characters "unhappy in their own way," "Lady with a Pet Dog" gets revisited not just by readers who love the Russian classics but by fiction writers who rewrite the text for their own time and place. Chekhov was reborn American in Joyce Carol Oates's famous 1972 story "The Lady and the Pet Dog" and received a new treatment by Michelle Herman in her 1998 novella *A New and Glorious Life*. Both American writers found Chekhov's plot irresistible: featuring beach scenes and walks in the woods, a vacation and an artist's retreat—like Chekhov's these works demonstrate the power of a "time out" and of a place where characters can reinvent themselves. Characters conceive of who they are and who they might seem to be, and in this resort setting they adjust to see what their other options might be.

Back in Yalta, as Dmitry and Anna continue their affair through part two of the story, they meet every day, eat lunch, stroll along the embankment, dine, admire the sea. The ability to be in public and yet somehow in private captivates them and us as readers. Seeing and being seen are essential parts of Yalta life. We've talked about how Anna Karenina and her sister-in-law Kitty were on display at that Moscow ball and at the train station—spa or vacation culture offers opportunities for the voyeur and simultaneously engenders a false sense of freedom.

> Their complete idleness, those kisses in broad daylight, with a furtive look around and the fear that someone might see them, the heat, the smell of the sea, and the constant flashing before their eyes of idle, smartly dressed, well-fed people, seemed to transform him: he repeatedly told Anna Sergeevna how beautiful she was, and how seductive, was impatiently passionate, never left her side, while she often brooded and kept asking him to admit that he did not respect her, did not love her at all, and saw in her a trite woman. Late almost every evening they went somewhere out of town, to Oreanda or the cascade; these outings were successful, their impressions each time were beautiful, majestic.

As readers, we understand that the "majestic" impressions may be more on his side than on hers, since she is brooding, concerned about her status as "other woman." But we have experienced the majesty ourselves in the sound picture painted of the Oreanda view.

Chekhov emphasizes the senses in this paragraph, and the words "the smell of the sea" evoke specific emotions in his readers, or perhaps fire readers' imaginations if they've never been to the sea. For Crimean Tatars, Georgians, Russians, and Ukrainians (as well as Bulgarians, Moldovans, Romanians, and Turks) who know the Black Sea, the scent may bring memories. Regardless, what Chekhov has done is to conjure the physical, so that even in translation we experience what is happening: the scent of the sea air, its stillness, the waves lapping in an eternal return. The verbal has become physical, and in that way the text echoes the characters' interactions. That is one of the pleasures of this prose.

For another famous traveler to the area, Mark Twain, who visited the emperor Alexander II in 1867 and commented on Yalta, it was the dramatic scenery, specifically the juxtaposition of mountains and water, that struck him, reminding him of home.

> We anchored here at Yalta, Russia, two or three days ago. To me the place was a vision of the Sierras. The tall, gray mountains that back it, their sides bristling with pines—cloven with ravines—here and there a hoary rock towering into view— long, straight streaks sweeping down from the summit to the sea, marking the passage of some avalanche of former times— all these were as like what one sees in the Sierras as if the one were a portrait of the other. The little village of Yalta nestles at the foot of an amphitheatre which slopes backward and upward to the wall of hills and looks as if it might have sunk quietly down to its present position from a higher elevation. This depression is covered with the great parks and gardens of noblemen, and through the mass of green foliage the bright colors of their palaces bud out here and there like flowers. It is a beautiful spot.

The theatrical metaphor of Twain's description—the amphitheatre of the mountain range above the town—reminds us of why Yalta was a perfect destination for Anton Chekhov the playwright, and the ideal setting for the extramarital affair he portrays in "Lady with a Pet Dog."

Twain's image of palaces "blooming" amid the green foliage of the hillside animates the landscape.

Chekhov moved to Crimea for its mild climate. He hadn't wanted to be so far from the capital and had to make his peace with Yalta once his health demanded that he relocate. Leaving his theatrical family behind in Moscow, Chekhov had to give up his dream of an "ensemble life." As he wrote to Grigory Rossolino, a doctor friend, on October 11, 1899, "I have been exiled to Yalta, a splendid exile perhaps, but still exile." What for Twain was inspiring and evocative became for Chekhov a gilded cage.

As a location, Yalta drew many tourists, and Chekhov's protagonists are barely aware that they must share these beautiful places with others. Vacation time and vacation spots are natural opportunities for lust, for short-term liaisons. Dmitry and Anna, to their own surprise and the surprise of readers, find that their torrid vacation romance has staying power and goes on to transform their lives forever. The "new and glorious life" they dream of is still ahead, and it has been made possible by that eternal indifference of the waves and the magnificent mountains that so impressed Twain.

Chekhov's pair meet and separate on that same Black Sea shore, returning to their respective homes in Moscow and the provincial town of S., places that are even more banal, meaningless, and gray after their Yalta sojourn. The protagonists' occupations and obligations away from the resort town are no less idle: Dmitry visits his club in Moscow, walks his daughter to school, and avoids conversing with his wife, while Anna Sergeevna sits in her house behind a gray fence or with the rest of what passes for society in S., attends the premiere of a play, *The Geisha*, that represents women as exoticized sexual objects. Anna's feeling that Dmitry must despise her as a "trite woman" during their affair in Yalta is mirrored in the performance hall of S., where the play features a trite woman who is observed by the trite citizens of the town. The town of S. itself has that pseudonym precisely because it is banal, every-provincial-town, not worth pinning down or treating to its own individual description. This Russian literary convention underlines the grayness of Anna's place of residence.

Why has this story had such staying power, in Russia and with foreign readerships? The contrast of culture and nature, the descriptions in their detailed specificity, must play a part, but more importantly perhaps the open ending, the Chekhovian lack of denouement, gives us pause. There is no answer to this dilemma— two people who spend time in a hotel room, married, but not to each other. Chekhov's description of them as "birds of passage caught and forced to live in separate cages" reminds us that the happier vacation time, in a place of last resort, gave the couple a bird's-eye view of the past, present, and future. Happiness, it turns out, is more complicated than spa life can support. It thrives on complexity, difficulty, even separation. The ending of this story suggests that the mere ability to go on, in the presence of love, can be enough.

Eternal Questions

When we talk about nineteenth-century Russian literature and social history, we highlight what the civic critics of the time called the "accursed questions": who is to blame, what is to be done, when will the real day come? Especially for students, the answers seem important. They can be reluctant to embrace ambiguity and the agency it gives us as readers. Regarding Chekhov, who embodied the turn of the century in Russia, I used to toss a question of my own at my literature students:

> Philosopher Lev Shestov famously wrote: 'Persistently, dolefully, monotonously, during his almost 25-year literary career, Chekhov was engaged in one single activity: the various ways to kill human hope.' Agree or disagree with Shestov.

Was he really killing hope? Certainly, those who find Chekhov boring or depressing would agree with Shestov. But what about those "birds of passage"? that "new and glorious life"? Surely the lack of finale in a Chekhov story or play implies that there is still hope: another dawn, another day, another opportunity for failure, melancholy, or lack of communication, but also for success, joy, connection? My Russian friend and colleague Andrei Stepanov says that in this well-known quote Shestov was not necessarily criticizing Chekhov but rather acknowledging Chekhov's ability to convey *more* than just ideological sentiments. Hope, it turns out, is not something one can kill. Chekhov lampooned those who thought you could, using for example the melodramatic character of Konstantin Treplev in *The Seagull* who kills a bird and throws it at the feet of his unrequited love. Birds of passage or a seagull can be symbols of flight, of freedom, of escape, but Chekhov held his characters to a higher standard, offering them the opportunity to take responsibility for their actions and to avoid thinking in overly simplistic binaries. My students, in their essay exams, have defended Chekhov from what they saw as Shestov's accusation—but they rarely claim to find Chekhov cheerful.

In his fiction, Chekhov wanted to show, not tell. (How many creative writing teachers have made that same point? They might as well print up t-shirts for their students: "Be Chekhovian!") He claimed that it was his duty to point out situations and portray human characters with all their faults, and it was up to the reader to come to conclusions. You might turn to Tolstoy or even Dostoevsky for the answers. Chekhov only has the questions. And that too is one of the pleasures of prose. I love a good narrative where all the ends tie up neatly, but I also really like to continue to think about the situations and characters I have met in a book. We get plenty of preaching and judgmental reactions in our daily lives. I can do without them in my reading.

It may be a stretch to write about Chekhov's drama as "prose," but as I tell my students, the only definition of prose is "not poetry," not arranged in lines on a page so as to look like a poem, whether rhymed or not. Chekhov's plays—most of which he characterized as "comedies"—have given us great characters, including the beleaguered Sonya of *Uncle Vanya* and her tedious but important proto-ecologist doctor friend Astrov, the actresses and writers of *The Seagull*, the entrepreneurial businessman, loyal old servant, and tragically bankrupt landowner of *The Cherry Orchard*. We'll look at some American reactions to the plays toward the end of this chapter.

First, though, I remind students that prose includes not only short stories, novels, and plays, but also travelogues, scientific articles, and letters—and Chekhov kept up an extensive correspondence. In this literary form, the personal letter, he was much less equivocal, not leaving the answers to his reader. Instead, not afraid of asserting his point of view, he became downright pedantic, especially toward his brothers. I give excerpts from the letters to my students as a way to offset any frustration they may have and to help them see the strong moral stance lurking behind Chekhov's narrator in the short stories.

Chekhov's letters differ significantly from his other prose. Rather than creating and animating literary characters, the letters illuminate his own character and delineate his own views—the sort we must hunt for in his fiction. My favorite of Chekhov's letters dates from March 1886. The author, just past his twenty-sixth birthday at the time, writes like an old man, scolding and instructing his younger brother about the proper way to live. I offer you only partial excerpts. In this long letter Anton explains to Nikolai what it means to be well-bred. "To my mind," Chekhov writes, "well-bred people ought to satisfy the following conditions:

1. They respect the individual and are therefore always indulgent, gentle, polite and compliant.
2. Their compassion extends beyond beggars and cats.
3. They respect the property of others and therefore pay their debts.
4. They are candid and fear lies like the plague. … They know how to keep their mouths shut and they do not force uninvited confidences on people.
5. They do not belittle themselves merely to arouse sympathy.
6. They are not preoccupied with vain things.
7. If they have talent, they respect it. They sacrifice comfort, women, wine and vanity to it. … What is more, they are fastidious.
8. They cultivate their aesthetic sensibilities."

And so on.

These are very specific criticisms of a specific person—and yes, they are preachy and judgmental. Anton goes on to advise his brother that it's time to change his ways.

> You must work at it constantly, day and night. You must never stop reading, studying in depth, exercising your will. Every hour is precious. ... Come home. Smash your vodka bottle, lie down on the couch and pick up a book. You might even give Turgenev a try. You've never read him. You must swallow your ... pride. You're no longer a child. You'll be thirty soon. It's high time!

Not for nothing is correspondence kept, published, translated. This is good advice for most of us! But why might we consider a book of Chekhov's letters as prose worth savoring? And how can Chekhov help us solve the eternal questions?

First, when we love a writer, we have that human curiosity of wanting to get to know him or her, to see and hear what s/he says to personal friends, to family. If a writer is good, that style—the descriptions and expressions, the structure and method of telling a story—will also be present in letters. Now, though, we are peering not into a created world (a world, in Lev Shestov's words, "created out of nothing"), but into the very world that *is* that nothing, the world that has shaped the author, given him or her words and phrases, intonations and ways of speaking, details of behaviors both admirable and scandalous. This is more than just peeking into the writer's workshop by looking over drafts and notebooks. Letters are completed, composed pieces of writing in and of themselves. A letter has a beginning, a middle, and an end; an addressee and a message; an attitude. It demonstrates the author's relationship with that addressee, and we can place ourselves in either position or just sit by and watch.

When Chekhov writes to his brothers, his sister, or his mother, to his publisher friends or other authors, he uses a combination of jocular expressions and more meaningful advice. He shows emotion, and also an awareness that emotion is not enough. (See above: the well-bred man.) About his father's death he writes to his brother Mikhail: "I knew what all of you had to go through at Father's funeral, and I felt vile inside." He goes on, sharing news of some land he's purchasing in Yalta and of the house he plans to build. "Constantly wandering around, moving from hotel to hotel, with their doormen and undependable food and so on and so forth is a frightening prospect." And the practical: "Mother could spend the winters with me."

> There is no winter here; it is late October and the roses and other flowers are outdoing one another with blossoms, the trees are green and the weather is warm. There's water everywhere you look. Nothing more than a house itself is needed here, no outbuildings, because everything is located under one roof. Coal, firewood, janitor's quarters and everything else is in the basement. Hens lay all year round, and they don't even need any special housing; a few partitions are enough. There is a bakery and a marketplace nearby. So it will be very warm and very comfortable for Mother. Incidentally, everyone gathers saffron milk caps and chanterelles in the State Forest all autumn long. That will keep Mother entertained.

Having been unable to travel to his father's funeral due to his own illness, Chekhov begins to plan for his mother's comfort, and for his own new life on a different, southern estate. (Unspoken in the letter remains the anxiety that he wants to get his mother settled because he knows his tuberculosis is incurable and that she will soon lose him as well.)

The details bring the space into being: creation of something out of nothing again. Chekhov's dislike of resort life—his gilded cage, where he is no "bird of passage"—is palpable, as is his desire to create a new home in Yalta, one that is "warm and comfortable." He is striving to adjust to new circumstances as best he can. Chekhov ends the letter with various greetings to others, but also with literary news: "My *Uncle Vanya* is making the rounds of the provinces and has been successful everywhere. You never know when you're going to win and when you're going to lose. I'd placed no hopes whatsoever on that play. Keep well and write."

I suppose that a book of an author's correspondence is even easier to "dip into" than a book of short stories. For a book of prose that you want to reread, to seek out precise descriptions, to write out a phrase or two to contemplate later, Chekhov's letters definitely fit the bill. I'll allow myself one more example. We love writers because of their writing, but also because of how they see the writing of others. In an otherwise very topical letter to Alexei Suvorin—Chekhov's friend and publisher—Chekhov explores a French novel that has been translated and is being published serially in the *Northern Herald*. (Suvorin has devoted several articles to the novel in his own journal.) Chekhov praises the author (Paul Bourget) and then points to his novel's fault: "his pretentious crusade against materialist doctrine." This gives Chekhov an opening to explain his own understanding of man and matter. "Materialism," Chekhov asserts,

> is not a school or doctrine ... neither chance occurrence nor passing fancy; it is something indispensable and inevitable and beyond human power. Everything that lives on earth is necessarily materialistic. ... Creatures of a higher order, thinking humans, are also necessarily materialists. They search for truth in matter because there is nowhere else for them to search: all they can see, hear and feel is matter. They can necessarily seek out truth only where their microscopes, probes and knives are effective. Prohibiting materialist doctrine is akin to preventing man from seeking out the truth.

Annoyed with the doctrinairely positivist attitude of the French novel, Chekhov cannot resist defending the scientific method. He ends this letter with an apology for his "philosophy." We read it and think: he is not killing hope at all, he is seeking truth, in his letters, his fiction, his plays.

One reason Chekhov can transport his readers, even as they read his letters, is his understanding of the deep connection between humanism and science, between the soul and the body. In a follow-up letter a week later Chekhov continues: "Different branches of knowledge have always lived together in peace. Both anatomy and belles-lettres are of equally noble descent. ... If a man knows the theory of the circulatory system, he is rich. If he learns the history of religion and the song 'I Remember a Marvelous Moment' in addition, he is the richer, not the poorer, for it."

The song Chekhov mentions is based on Pushkin's short lyrical poem from 1827, and in it Pushkin described a moment in which the spiritual and the physical meet, a moment that can be as transformative as religion. In his letter Chekhov evokes the poetic image without quoting it, but for any Russian reader the reference is clear. This "marvelous moment" captured a "genius of pure beauty," a woman in Pushkin's life who was acting here as a muse. By connecting this idea to the working of the circulatory system Chekhov becomes the darling of medical humanities—demonstrating that poetry and science inform in complementary ways.

The Nexus of Physical and Spiritual

One reason some say they like Russian literature is because they appreciate the "Russian soul." I don't have a lot of patience for such talk (it seems imprecise, banal, vague, and also slightly culturally offensive somehow, to Russians and to the rest of us, who are what, *without* a soul?), but I do find the way Chekhov explores the nexus of the physical and spiritual to be compelling. We could pick any of his stories as evidence, but the 1892 story "Ward No. 6" works particularly well. This portrayal of the state of Russian medical and psychiatric care has influenced writers and filmmakers across the world, and it also stands beside Chekhov's letter to his brother Nikolai as an example of how Chekhov portrays the ethics of living well.

The story's protagonist, Dr. Andrei Ragin, presides over a provincial hospital. Although he resents being far away from the exciting life and professional opportunities of the capital, Ragin is able to find a comfortable rhythm. He sees his patients, of course, and he subscribes to medical journals, but he also likes a glass of beer in the afternoon and a philosophical chat. The story, which unfolds slowly, turns out to be an indictment of bureaucracy and self-delusion. Having decided upon arriving in the town that the hospital at which he is to serve is "an immoral institution and extremely hazardous to the health of the townspeople," Dr. Ragin also determines that he cannot swim against the tide. He does not take any action to rectify the situation. While not a bad person per se, he allows his weak will and his passivity to lead to great evil in the space of the town.

Composed of nineteen very short chapters, the story takes Chekhov's readers into the ward before even introducing the doctor. Part I opens with a description of the physical environment and gradually turns into a tour: we observe the "annex" surrounded by a forest of weeds and separated from the field beyond by a "gray hospital fence with nails on top." For the reader of "Lady with a Pet Dog," this fence recalls Anna Sergeevna's gray home in her gray provincial town, but now it evokes as well, in the narrator's words, the "godforsaken look" of Russian hospitals and prisons. Before any patients come into view, we see the old guard Nikita with his "huge fists" who belongs, we are told, to that class of people who believe in beatings.

The psych ward itself has the stench of a menagerie … and the reader meets each inmate in turn as if visiting animals in their cages. These "lunatics," like zoo animals, are each of a specific and different type: a sad and grieving consumptive; the Jew Moisei, who regularly goes out begging and comes back to a beating; a fat peasant who is paralyzed; and a gentleman named Ivan Dmitrich Gromov who suffers from persecution mania. In fact, there are five inmates, but Gromov is so interesting that the narrator gets distracted for some pages before remembering to identify the fifth, a tradesman and former mail sorter who seems to be stuck on the medals and awards he thinks he is achieving. (We finally learn a bit about the fifth patient some eight pages in, in chapter four of the story.) In Dr. Ragin's empire, where no one but the barber ventures anymore, and that only every few months, the rude and unscrupulous Nikita reigns supreme. This leisurely perusal ends with a surprising statement. "It is rumored that the doctor has begun to visit Ward No. 6."

Russian readers at the time recognized the opening pages in particular as fitting a familiar genre, that of the "physiological sketch." Popular in England and France in the 1830s and 1840s, this journalism-infused genre offered a view into specific social classes, their lives, values, conditions. Chekhov follows his predecessor Dostoevsky in using it to bring us closer to his characters and to remind us that we are all human, we can all suffer. This story represented Chekhov's indictment of the provinces, of tsarist-era bureaucrats and their incompetence, and it was a galvanizing motivation for action and reform. For readers in translation today, the details of horrors faced in this provincial medical institution underline our own fears—of being left out of contemporary science, of being at the mercy of those in charge who may or may not be competent, of unnecessary physical and psychological pain, inflicted through deliberate viciousness, thoughtless neglect, or our own inabilities to navigate the modern medical and insurance systems. Some people indulge in science fiction or watch slasher films, but for me there is nothing so awful and terrifying, and so likely to spur to action, as Chekhov's detailed descriptions of callous apathy. Could it be that only *those* people lacked empathy, in Russia, back in the day, not now, in our society, today? We know that's not true. In Chekhov we see an indictment of social conditions—in the United States, the UK, India, Brazil, in the past and in the twenty-first century—that allow structural rigidity and incompetence to prevent humane attitudes toward our fellow citizens.

Perhaps the above lays it on a bit thick. Why *would* we want to read "Ward No. 6" today? Chekhov is among several famed Russian writer-doctors, and his works are read for insight into systems, medical, pedagogical, and institutional. His oft-quoted statement that "medicine is my wife, and literature is my mistress" helps consider how those two métiers resemble each other. Description and diagnosis are important for both writers and doctors, and for many readers diagnosis, and self-diagnosis, have become a full-time hobby. Some doctors, like Sigmund Freud, long to become writers. Some, like Chekhov—and his countrymen Vikenty Veresaev (1867–1945), Mikhail Bulgakov (1891–1940), and Maxim Osipov (born 1963)—do.

Recently a former student contacted me to mention that she's been thinking about "Ward No. 6," which she read with me in a course I call *Madness and Power in Russia*. "Looking at mental illness from a humanities perspective," she wrote, "has influenced how I see the clinical skills and therapeutic interventions I've been learning as I train as a mental health therapist." Chekhov's descriptions indict the doctor, who is a representative of earthly power and who had the knowledge and the means to engage in therapeutic intervention, but chose not to. He also indicts the tsarist system. Systems organize how the world functions, but they also distort. As individuals we often feel helpless in the face of bureaucracy, or as we watch from afar the horrors of war, poverty, discrimination. Dr. Ragin had the authority and agency to combat the tragedy in the hospital next door, and yet he was too lazy or indifferent to wield his own power, to disturb the status quo. Chekhov makes him pay—and he enables his readers to remain empathetic and to learn from the story in part by evoking our pity for the doctor as well as for his patients.

The Play's the Thing

A book of short stories can be dipped into, and it can be thrown into a suitcase or even a coat pocket. Short stories take us into another world, someone else's life, a new locale. A short story is an escape, but it's not a commitment—perhaps like that vacation on the shores of the Black Sea. For readers and writers of short stories in English, Chekhov's popularity is almost unseemly. In the English-speaking world the descriptor "Chekhovian" guarantees a great short story, and thus Chekhov, and others who write in his vein, continue to attract a broad readership.

Chekhov is also the most produced playwright in English after Shakespeare. Put another way, more Chekhov plays are staged in English than any other non-English writer; he is the most produced playwright in translation. And yet his plays are about Russian country estates and country doctors, about standing military regiments and provincial schoolteachers and telegraph operators—hardly the stuff of contemporary life. What is it about Chekhov's plays that makes them so popular—and can we argue that they too show us the pleasures of prose?

To do so, I want to venture into other areas of literary production, into scripts and theatrical productions and films, all of which demonstrate how Chekhov remains relevant, even when his works are set decades in the past and in locales completely foreign to us. The reasons we read include desires to escape, to travel, to experience new vistas, but we remember what we read for entirely other reasons, primarily because the characters have entered our emotional universe.

Not everyone has access to professional theater—as I well know from my perch in the Ohio countryside—but it's possible to produce a Chekhov play once and have it reverberate for years when you put it on screen. I'm reminded here of the titular character of the film *Educating Rita* (1983) who when asked by her tutor how to make a Shakespeare play timely and help it reach a broader audience replied (cue British accent here) "Put it on the radio." In fact, Chekhov's stories have great success on the radio, particularly on the American National Public Radio show "Selected Shorts," where famous actors read dramatically and humorously to the delight of in-person live audiences and distanced ones listening anywhere in the world the NPR app reaches. In addition, many films have been made from Chekhov plays. One of the most interesting is by film director Louis Malle. It started as a project of Andre Gregory, who rehearsed Chekhov on and off for a number of years with friends and then invited his mate Louis Malle to bring *Uncle Vanya* to the big screen in the 1994 film *Vanya on 42nd Street*.

What I love about this film is the seamless opening. We see people—regular people as well as familiar character actors along with Gregory, the production director—walking along a New York street, with the taxis honking and the general bustle of busy city life all around them. The actors begin to greet each other, to chat, and to enter an abandoned New Amsterdam theater building, where some take a seat in the auditorium while others climb onto the stage and … begin the play. You don't even notice when actor Larry Pine is suddenly Dr. Astrov. And yet he is. The lines he begins to speak are transformative, and without costumes or props, the actors transport us into Chekhov's Russia.

Chekhov's *Uncle Vanya* chronicles the end of an age and a crisis on an estate, but what we have seen in the opening minutes of Malle's film reminds us that when things seem to be falling apart, they sometimes gain new life. The setting in the theater-turned-movie palace, shuttered in 1982, with its cobwebs and general feeling of decay and neglect, reinforces the feeling of fin de siècle integral to Chekhov's play. The production progresses slowly, with intimate conversations and laughter, tears and hysteria, declaimed monologues and dismissive interruptions. With no playbill in our hands, no cast of characters or list of scenes and acts, we are plunged into this long-disappeared world as if it were our own.

There have been other film versions and adaptations of Chekhov's plays, including one that set the action in Australia. But I want to pause for a moment on a New York-inspired film that also features *Uncle Vanya*, Sasha Cohen Waters's 2010 *Chekhov for Children*. As Waters describes it, she was a youngish filmmaker when someone sent her an old VHS tape of a theater production that was staged at Symphony Space in New York City by none other than her fifth- and sixth-grade classmates, children who had been corralled into exploring and putting on Chekhov by the writer Phillip Lopate.

Lopate had a residency with a New York City public school arts program in 1979 and chose this play, in his words, in an effort to share "Chekhov's lessons on miscommunication and irony" with his young students. In her film, which she shapes into four acts like a Chekhov play, Waters explores the filmmaking process—she was videographer rather than an actor in the elementary school production—and also reconnects with her classmates to see how their lives, thirty years later, have mirrored or contradicted the storylines predicted by the Chekhov characters they played as children.

In their projects Waters and Lopate (who wrote a well-known essay, also entitled "Chekhov for Children," about the experience) explore the nature of childhood and meditate on age more generally. Waters points out that Chekhov was thirty-nine when he wrote Uncle Vanya. Lopate was thirty-seven when he worked with the P.S. 75 children, and the filmmaker just a tad older when she reengaged with her childhood experience. "When one is forty," she writes, "one knows that at age ten, virtually all mistakes are reversible; but when one is ten, one is unlikely to possess such hard-won, adult wisdom." What could it have meant for these children to engage with Chekhov's words, his dialogues, his characters' inability to hear or speak to each other? How did standing on stage talking about the weather in Chekhov's words evoke their parents and teachers, who probably stood around talking about the weather a lot of the time, and predict their own future need to endure weather that no one ever seems to be able to do anything about? People sometimes complain that Chekhov plays are boring, that nothing happens, but these children were able to find the something behind the nothing.

To give just two examples, Waters's classmate Angus played the titular Uncle Vanya, and for him the project of adapting a classic text into a version that spoke to the children was a revelation. The play, he recalled, defined the concept of a "living document," one that retained its meaning "across cultures and generations." Angus would go on to become a history professor and he credits Chekhov with helping to "unlock a performative aspect" of his personality. Another classmate, whom Waters recalls as being particularly "sweet-faced," channeled his grouchy Uncle Oscar to portray the Professor, and although as an adult David questioned whether they had really "got the depth" of the play, his later career as a commercial photographer who specializes in portraiture, particularly of children, suggests that at some time in his youth he learned how to see into people. Lopate noted that while working with the text, the children regularly noticed the inability of Chekhov's characters to connect and communicate. It felt ironic to them to work through the lines of characters who failed to listen to each other.

Lopate believed that "we are twelve years old and we are already who we are going to be. It's like a photograph being developed, it just becomes clearer and clearer, and that's what interests me, that character is destiny." But is it? Waters resists the idea that at ten she knew she would become a filmmaker, but she recognizes in her current self the habits of a much younger person. She definitely agrees that the opportunity to engage with Chekhov, to embrace creative expression, was "foundational." In 2012 Waters wrote:

> The students involved in Lopate's production of Uncle Vanya are today a public defender-turned-Newbery Award-winning

author; a Paris-based hip-hop performer; a professor of filmmaking in the Midwest … ; an historian; a community activist; a photographer; a family therapist; an entertainment industry consultant, and the highest-ranking black woman in the New York state governor's office. All of us work in creative or public service fields, or both.

Proud of her classmates? Of course. For us as readers of Waters and as viewers of her documentary film, performance, performing Chekhov's words and adapting them along the way to their ten-year-old understanding, seems to offer that same view into the past, present and future that the Black Sea at Oreanda offered in "Lady with a Pet Dog."

This is not the place to lament the reorientation of American education away from the "great books," arts programming, and foreign language access of my childhood. But the view into 1970s public education in New York City does remind us that when children encounter great literature, it affects them, and it can remain relevant throughout their lives. My own love of Chekhov stems from what I recall as an endless production of one of Chekhov's less famous plays, *Ivanov*, at my own public high school. I attended the play as an eight-year-old, and though I know I snoozed through some of it, I also remember being intrigued with the language, the conversations and monologues and outfits of these characters from another world, strolling across the stage and endlessly drinking tea, even as they were portrayed by teenagers in the Chicago suburbs.

Chekhov takes us inside institutions like Ward No. 6, but also inside theaters, hotels, and schools, inside marriages and other kinds of relationships, inside tropes like the seaside vacation or teatime at a country estate or a funeral. His characters live those relationships, those roles, those places. They take us with them into these masterpieces of prose. We glimpse their truths while also meditating on our own. That is part of why we read—to explore the experiences of others and to think more deeply about our lives.

I'm not sure I could be as brave as Phillip Lopate and try to bring Chekhov to ten- and twelve-year-olds. I do know, though, that reading

Chekhov is a lifetime endeavor. Revisiting his stories, plays, and letters with my students or on my own, I am able to consider the human predicament, the whole array of human predicaments, that make his time relevant for mine.

As the title of this book admits, the question of "needing Russian literature" has become more fraught in recent months and years. But I think we (still) need it. Russian history has always been filled with aggressive actions and tragic results. And the war being waged on its neighbor Ukraine in the early 2020s (or to be more precise, since 2014) has highlighted those historical tendencies and brought them into the twenty-first century. But even as in some corners of the world people have talked about "cancelling" Russian culture or have argued that Russian books and their authors are to blame for the country's poor choices, I want to remember that Russia has rarely had a government honest people would embrace. Tsar Ivan IV, better known in English as "Ivan the Terrible," with his *oprichnina* and his vengeful attacks, like the 1570 massacre in the city of Novgorod? Peter I, who expanded his empire at the expense of the Finns and other neighboring peoples and who according to legend participated in the cellar torture of his own son? Or Joseph Stalin, whose government in the 1920s and 1930s caused incalculable suffering during the famine-inducing collectivization campaign and the parallel politically motivated arrests, repressions, executions, and hard labor sentences that formed part of the so-called Great Terror? Russian politics and even the cultural effects of authoritarian governments were outside the scope of this study, but I would note that in Russia over the decades authors themselves had plenty of problems with the Russian regime(s). Their writing speaks to us anyway ... or perhaps exactly because of those conflicts and complications.

AFTERWORD

In this little book I have mostly taken my readers through those nineteenth-century mainstream Russian authors, all men, whose works have been translated into English and many other languages and who are included on all the lists of "greatest hits." There is a reason, as I've tried to argue, that we should continue to read these books, stories, plays. The plots in many cases have become iconic, and they or variations thereon appear in texts of all kinds—literary, musical, film, stage—all over the globe. Although the worlds described in books by Pushkin, Dostoevsky, Tolstoy, and Chekhov have mostly disappeared, they remain relevant in all sorts of ways, and the experience of diving into the pages of these fictional works is still as transformative as it ever was.

Returning to these books over and over at different times of our lives gives us new insight into human nature and the nature of relationships. This short reading list, if we can call it that, offers opportunities to step outside our everyday setting and learn to empathize with other ways of living, other ways of thinking. We return to our own lives enriched, ourselves looking more closely at the details of daily life, the systems—political, institutional, social—that organize them, the ways we can interact with those around us. Like Sonya in Chekhov's *Uncle Vanya*, we are kinder to each other, and like Dostoevsky's Dunya Raskolnikova, we are ready to harness our intelligence and passion to the tasks at hand. We are also on the lookout for those precious, unexpected, glowing moments that may occur in life and can seek to make the most of them in personal and productive ways.

These authors are all men, but they represent very different social backgrounds and thus show us completely different realms across these and their many other works: an idealized life in the Russian countryside, and its upper-class urban counterpart; travel within Russia and beyond, including everything from German spas to Russian forests filled with mushrooms and berries; poverty and desperation in overheated slum-like conditions; and both the edges of the Russian empire (Crimea, Sakhalin Island) and its depths—provincial towns, agricultural estates, endless steppes. In the texts I've been able to write about here we have touched on only some of this.

My argument has been that *Russia* in particular, especially the Russian empire, gives us a vast diversity of human experience, and these talented writers—with their descriptive abilities, their psychological insights, their deep empathy—bring us into close proximity with the characters and places they depict.

Just as importantly, the literary techniques these authors employ, mostly from the realist tradition, captivate readers at all ages. Embedded in and engaged with European literary practices, the writers are constantly in dialogue with other authors, including but not limited to each other, and with their societies. One example might be the novel of adultery. Frequently we think of *Anna Karenina* in the context of Gustave Flaubert's *Madame Bovary* or Kate Chopin's *The Awakening*, but Tolstoy also had Pushkin in mind as he began his influential novel. What might have happened had Pushkin's heroine Tatiana not resisted the temptation to reignite her love for Eugene despite her changed status as a married woman? Some forty years after the publication of *Eugene Onegin*, Tolstoy shows us. Chekhov, too, is thinking of his predecessors when he allows Anna Sergeevna, the "lady with the pet dog," to violate her marital vows. He mirrors Tolstoy's tragic novel, and yet he veers in an entirely different direction, giving his heroine and his readers hope for the future.

These texts are significant for Russians, but also for writers and readers across the globe. They tackle the real human questions of matches and mismatches, of loyalty and fidelity, and of self-actualization and the chance to choose one's own destiny in what in nineteenth-century Russia—and not only there and then—is clearly a misogynist world.

Returning to Pushkin—to the beginning of the Russian literary tradition, of this book, of my "Masterpieces of Russian Literature" course—I might say that an essential reason we need Russian literature today is that it is not only serious, it can also be playful. And although I myself tend to love historical fiction and socially relevant novels, there is so much more to read and explore in the Russian tradition. For that reason, I want to end my argument with a brief appendix that will offer all kinds of different Russian fiction for readers who want more. Thank you for coming along on this journey. It's been a delight for me.

APPENDIX: MORE BOOKS TO READ

As a professor of Russian literature, I'm often asked what the best translations of this or that work are. I wish there were a quick and easy answer. Best is hard to judge, so I generally note that even good translations of imaginative prose can differ profoundly, depending on when or for whom they were published, with what emphasis or skill, and most actually still have something of value. Older translations take us into another era; up-to-date ones sometimes miss the mark or are too specific, say to an American audience. Obviously no one wants me to expound on these complexities when they ask me about translation. They just want suggestions as to what to read.

Rather than launch into comparisons of translations of the classics, I find it more productive to recommend new authors people may not have tried or even heard of—and when I do, I end up with long lists of unexpected works that will reward readers in unusual ways. Here I'm just going to go alphabetically through some of my favorite recommendations, with a couple words about each to tempt readers. I hope you will try at least some of them. They all remain surprisingly important.

Akhmatova, Anna (1889–1966): A Silver Age poet who lived long enough past the mid-twentieth century to influence Joseph Brodsky, Akhmatova's most poignant poem cycle tackles the Stalinist repressions. *Requiem* documents levels of grief and the horror of women left to mourn the arrested and executed. (She also wrote love poetry, if that's more your thing.)

Alexievich, Svetlana (born 1948): A recent Nobel prizewinner, Belarusian journalist Aleksievich interviews survivors—soldiers, children, mothers, post-Soviet citizens finding their way in a new world. Best is her *Unwomanly Face of War*, but I also love *Second-Hand*

Time, a book featuring post-Soviet stories that helps to understand those left behind in times of rapid historical change.

Babel, Isaac (1894–1940): Vivid stories of Ukraine, including life in Odessa, are matched by funny, tender, tragic chronicles of the civil war in his cycle *The Red Cavalry*. Babel's alter-ego, the newspaperman Liutov, tries to fit in with the Cossack soldiers with whom he's embedded while recognizing how traditional Jewish life is doomed in the Soviet era.

Brodsky, Joseph (1940–1996): Another Nobel prizewinner, Brodsky was arrested as a young man in the Soviet Union for being unemployed and famously stated that he wasn't unemployed at all: his profession was poetry. Exiled first to the north of Russia and eventually expelled from the USSR, Brodsky had a second act in the United States. I really love some of his essays, including the autobiographical "In a Room and a Half" about growing up in Leningrad (check out the biopic based on it), and especially his book of essays, *Watermark*, which focuses on two cities laced with canals, Venice and St. Petersburg.

Bulgakov, Mikhail (1881–1940): This one is easy. *Master and Margarita*, Bulgakov's so-called sunset novel, captivates most people, from teenaged boys to retirees. A twinned novel about the devil coming to Moscow in the 1930s and a Moscow author who has written a narrative set in ancient times (about Christ and Pontius Pilate), there are hijinks and history to spare in this book—and a mushroom-eating, walking, and talking giant cat to boot. Most famous quote? Probably "Manuscripts don't burn," a thought that has been small comfort indeed for generations of repressed Soviet and post-Soviet writers.

Bunin, Ivan (1870–1953): Also a Nobel prizewinner, Bunin wrote lyrical prose about the Russian countryside, about Moscow, about life abroad. Probably the best-traveled of any Russian author, he fled the Bolsheviks at the age of fifty and spent the rest of his life in France. Among my favorite of his stories are "In Paris," a short surprising tale about two exhausted émigrés who find love, and lose it, and a much earlier text about Moscow, "Mitya's Love," which details a young man's frustration as his own first love slips away.

Chukovskaya, Lydia (1907–1996): Daughter of a famous literary man, Chukovskaya herself writes haunting prose, including her parody of a socialist realist novel about a woman whose son is arrested during the Great Terror. A wonderful companion piece to Akhmatova's *Requiem, Sofya Petrovna* is told from the point of view of a woman who believes in the rightness of the Soviet government—until she can no longer believe.

Dovlatov, Sergei (1941–1990): Forced to leave the Soviet Union, Dovlatov penned hilarious stories lampooning Soviet life and its paradigms, and his émigré fiction plays with tropes and clichés to offer insights into nostalgia. Never lachrymose, his stories have a tongue-in-cheek quality that belies the tragic life courses they often describe.

Gladkov, Fyodor (1883–1958): This Socialist Realist author told a compelling story of post-Civil War rebuilding in his novel *Cement*. Yes, it's about trying to bring a ruined cement factory back to life, but it also features young Communists, bureaucrats, engineers, mothers— all figures who struggle to come to terms with or contribute to the new Soviet world. Colorful, especially in its earliest English translation that preserves all the juicy (and feminist) bits that Gladkov would come to self-censor out over the decades.

Gogol, Nikolai (1809–1852): One of the central figures of nineteenth-century Russian prose, Gogol was actually from Ukraine and has been reclaimed by that country as their own. His writing has a specific Ukrainian cast to it, and I can recommend the stories in his collections *Evenings on a Farm near Dikanka* and *Mirgorod*, both set in Ukraine. His Petersburg tales include "The Nose" and "The Overcoat," vivid satires of that bureaucratic imperial city immortalized further in opera and film, and of course his famous novel is *Dead Souls*, a long picaresque journey through an imagined Russian countryside. Lean on plot, the novel teems with characters and colorful descriptions that make it a rollicking read.

Goncharov, Ivan (1812–1891): An American writer I know told me that the novel *Oblomov* changed his life when he was eighteen— he found the prose that compelling. I loved his reaction to a novel I like to advertise to my students as the story of a man so lazy, or perhaps just indecisive, that he doesn't even get out of bed for the first hundred pages of the book. Considered in its day an indictment of the system of serfdom, it treats its protagonist so gently that he becomes absolutely endearing.

Griboedov, Alexander (1792–1829): Known as a one-work author, Griboedov actually composed poetry, travel notes, music, and even economic projects as well as plays over the course of his relatively short life. *Woe from Wit*, his masterpiece, demonstrates the hypocrisy of Moscow society in the early nineteenth century. Many of its lines have become aphorisms in Russian, which makes it even harder than most verse drama to translate, but that doesn't stop people from trying. I'm expecting another new translation to come out in the next few years.

Grossman, Vasily (1905–1964): Another Jewish writer who has been embraced as one of the best authors to write about the triple tragedy of Stalinism, the Holocaust, and the Second World War. Grossman was a war correspondent who was the first to publish news of the atrocities at Treblinka. His novel *Life and Fate*, originally smuggled out of the Soviet Union on microfilm and published in Switzerland, features among other scenes an imagined version of the Nazi destruction of his hometown in Soviet Ukraine. Grossman's early story "In the Town of Berdichev" was made into the compelling film *Commissar*, censored in 1967 when it was completed but finally released at the end of the Soviet period.

Il'f and Petrov: These are the pseudonyms of Ilya Faynzilberg (1897–1937) and Evgeny Kataev (1902–1942), comic writers, Jews originally from Odessa, and beloved by Soviet and former Soviet citizens for their satiric take on the 1920s, a time of economic and social change that led to the terrifying Stalinist era. *The Twelve Chairs* follows a con artist, Ostap Bender, who teams up with a former nobleman seeking treasure hidden in the family dining room chairs by his mother-in-law. Made into a Hollywood as well as a Soviet film, the novel is better in its literary form. Laughing to myself while reading the novel on a train across the Urals, I was actually taken for a real Russian.

Khodasevich, Vladislav (1886–1939): One of Khodasevich's masterpieces is a biography of the eighteenth-century Russian poet and statesman Gavrila Derzhavin, and his *Necropolis* features brilliant personal essays about deceased contemporaries, but Khodasevich is really a fantastic if often melancholy classical poet, and there is even a wonderful bilingual collection of his verses available for the curious. I highly recommend this twentieth-century poet who fled Bolshevik Russia in 1922 and died relatively young in Paris.

Khvoshchinskaya, Sofia (1824–1865): *City Folk and Country Folk* is a charming novel that offers a woman's view into nineteenth-century estate life, for a change. Lovers of Goncharov or Ivan Turgenev will find the prose vivid and the point of view snappy. Expect more offerings by this author, her sisters, and other women of the era to become available as scholars and translators try to rebalance the literary world that seemed to lack women altogether before Akhmatova.

Makanin, Vladimir (1937–2017): This novelist from the Ural region started life as a mathematician, and his fiction explores his own sense of belonging both to Europe and to Asia. Because he wrote primarily in the late Soviet era (his first novel was published in 1966), Makanin is a great place to look for repercussions of life under repressive regimes. The psychological conditions in *The Escape Hatch* and *Baize-Covered Table with Decanter* (my two favorites) are crushing but utterly authentic.

Nabokov, Vladimir (1899–1977): American or Russian novelist? Nabokov belongs to the Russian tradition no matter what language he writes in, and I recommend reading the translated novels alongside the ones composed in English. I love *Luzhin's Defense*, a "chess novel" from the Russian-language European years (but don't watch the bad American film based on it), and *Pnin*, an academic novel whose hero is the sweetest character Nabokov ever created, but of course everyone should also read *Lolita*. One of my former advisors, Alexander Dolinin, has just written a 900-page commentary to *The Gift*, and that fabulous novel is complicated enough that you may want to wait until those commentaries are translated into English to tackle it for yourself.

Nikitin, Alexei (born 1967): This Russophone Ukrainian writer lives in Kyiv today, and his fiction is only now being translated into English. Look for *Victory Park* which should be out by 2024, a novel of the 1980s, those complicated years during *perestroika* when Soviet culture (and economics) were imploding, but new national consciousnesses were not yet arising. Contrast it with *The Face of Fire*, in the tradition of Grossman and also due out soon. Based on the author's own family history, the sprawling historical novel chronicles the Second World War across Ukraine and shows Ukrainians, Jews, Russians, and more trying to survive—in some cases betraying friends and countrymen to save their own skins. Both novels are among the best I've read this century.

Osipov, Maxim (born 1963): Another of the Russian medical authors, Osipov has lived in a provincial town and practiced medicine as a cardiologist. He also has found wonderful translators who bring his particular diagnosis of contemporary Russian life to a global audience. *Rock, Paper, Scissors* gives a good sense of his short fiction. Osipov is the doctor Chekhov's Ragin ("Ward No. 6") should have been.

Pelevin, Viktor (born 1962): The darling of Russian post-modernism, Pelevin brings together pop culture, historical tropes, computer games, poetry, science, philosophy, and Soviet reality. My favorite is *Chapaev and Emptiness*, also published as *Buddha's Little Finger*, where early Soviet Russia is "rhymed" with the early 1990s, but I love *The Yellow Arrow* too, a novella that uses train travel to confront the disaster that was the Soviet system hurtling toward an inevitable abyss. *Omon Ra* seems to be a sci-fi or fantasy novel but is actually almost a straightforward chronicle of Soviet (and post-Soviet) obsessions with the Second World War and military achievement more broadly, including the space race.

Petrushevskaya, Lyudmila (born 1938): This fantastic novelist and playwright had a horrific childhood, and she emerged from it with a biting sense of humor and an unparalleled ear for Soviet voices. Her novella *The Time: Night* has been seen as an indictment of the broken Soviet matriarchal family, and while bleak, it is also very funny.

Shalamov, Varlam (1907–1982): New, more accurate translations into English of Shalamov's stories of the Stalinist Siberian labor camps have recently become available, and they are telling and poignant. No question that the subject matter is hard, but Shalamov's vivid imagery offers a window into true physical suffering as well as a necessary supplement to Solzhenitsyn's *Gulag Archipelago*.

Solzhenitsyn, Alexander (1918–2008): In the 1970s and early 1980s everyone was reading thick paperback copies of *The*

Gulag Archipelago, the book that got Solzhenitsyn kicked out of the Soviet Union. But his little novella *One Day in the Life of Ivan Denisovich*—actually published in the Soviet Union in 1962 during the so-called cultural "Thaw," with Nikita Khrushchev's express approval—portrays the conditions of Siberian labor camps with less drama and more humanity. This Nobel prizewinner has numerous thick historical novels to choose from, but *One Day* is probably his masterpiece.

Turgenev, Ivan (1818–1883): Recently a student of mine decided to read all of Turgenev on his own, and he reported loving every novel. *Fathers and Children* is the classic, but *Rudin*, one of his first, has a heroine to rival Pushkin's Tatiana. Stronger, smarter, more independent. In a novel by a man! If you keep your eye out, you might be able to see a contemporary staged performance of Turgenev's play *A Month in the Country*—perhaps put on by companies who love Chekhov but want a new challenge. Turgenev's lyrical book of stories, *Notes of a Hunter* (the title has many different translations), definitively showed Russian readers that peasants were human beings too.

Tynianov, Yuri (1894–1943): How can I not mention this wonderful historical novelist who was a key figure in my first book? I've mentioned him earlier, where I talk about him as a literary scholar, but Tynianov wrote stories as well as biographical fiction. You may know the Prokofiev piece written on themes from his novella *Lieutenant Kizhe*, and I also recommend *The Death of Vazir-Mukhtar*, a modernist novel about the last year in the life of Griboedov, the poet-diplomat who was killed in Tehran in 1829.

Ulitskaya, Lyudmila (born 1943): Another contemporary woman writer, Ulitskaya shows us the multiethnic historically complex layers of Crimea in her novel *Medea and Her Children*. I especially like the short stories in which she plumbs the depths of family life, particularly in the difficult post–Second-World-War years, but you might also enjoy *The Funeral Party*, a book I put on the reading list of my hypothetical undergraduate course entitled "The Happy Russian Novel." Sometimes I joke that a course like that would draw a lot of students, because its reading list would be so short, but in fact I remain hopeful that Russian (and Russophone) life will change enough in the twenty-first century—after this war ends—that there may be many more such texts penned in future.

Vail and Genis: Pyotr Vail (1949–2009) and Alexander Genis (born 1953) wrote as a team even after they fled the Soviet Union until eventually parting ways. Vail (born in Riga, Latvia) then lived in Czechoslovakia while Genis (born in Ryazan, Russia) still lives in New York. Their writing is filled with nostalgia for their lost homeland, but with that special Russian-language touch that is sharp and biting and so very perceptive. I translated their *Russian Cuisine in Exile* with my student Tom some years back, and the edition has three things to recommend it: hilarious essays, useful cooking advice, and gorgeous (mostly) Soviet-era illustrations (mostly) from the mother of all Soviet cookbooks, *The Book of Tasty and Healthy Food*, first published in 1939. Enjoy.

WORKS CITED AND
CONSULTED

Bayley, John. *Tolstoy and the Novel* (London: Chatto & Windus, 1966).

Batuman, Elif. *The Possessed: Adventures with Russian Books and the People Who Read Them* (New York: Farrar, Straus and Giroux, 2010).

Berlin, Isaiah. *The Hedgehog and the Fox: An Essay on Tolstoy's View of History* (New York: Simon and Schuster, 1966).

Brintlinger, Angela. "Writing about Madness: Russian Attitudes toward Psyche and Psychiatry, 1887–1907." In *Madness and the Mad in Russian Culture*, ed. Angela Brintlinger and Ilya Vinitsky (Toronto: University of Toronto Press, 2007), 173–91.

Broom, Timothy W., Robert S. Chavez, and Dylan D. Wagner. "Becoming the King in the North: Identification with Fictional Characters Is Associated with Greater Self–Other Neural Overlap." *Social Cognitive and Affective Neuroscience*, 16 (6), June 2021: 541–51.

Burry, Alexander, and Frederick H. White, eds. *Border Crossing: Russian Literature into Film* (Edinburgh: Edinburgh University Press, 2016).

Chekhov, Anton. *Anton Chekhov's Life and Thought: Selected Letters and Commentary*, translated by Michael Henry Heim, notes by Simon Karlinsky (Berkeley: University of California Press, 1975).

Chekhov, Anton. To Mikhail Chekhov, Yalta, October 25, 1898, 328–30.

Chekhov, Anton. To Nikolai Chekhov, Moscow, March 1886, 48–51.

Chekhov, Anton. To Alexei Suvorin, Sumy, May 7, 1889, 143–5.

Chekhov, Anton. To Alexei Suvorin, Sumy, May 15, 1889, 145–7.

Chizh, Vladimir. *Dostoevsky as "Psychopathologist": An Essay* (Moscow: University Typography, 1885). In Russian.

Clayton, Douglas. *Ice and Flame: Aleksandr Pushkin's Eugene Onegin* (Toronto: University of Toronto Press, 1985).

de Sherbinin, Julie. "American Iconography of Chekhov." In *Chekhov the Immigrant: Translating a Cultural Icon*, ed. Michael C. Finke and Julie de Sherbinin (Bloomington, IN: Slavica, 2007), 103–26.

Dickinson, Sara. "Nineteenth Century Russian Literature and the Shaping of *Lolita*." In *Critical Insights: Lolita*, ed. Rachel Stauffer (Ipswich, MA: Salem Press, 2016).

Works Cited and Consulted

Dostoevsky, Fyodor. *Crime and Punishment* (1866), trans. Jessie Coulson & ed. George Gibian (New York: Norton, 1989).

Emerson, Caryl. "Chekhov and the Annas: Rewriting Tolstoy," reprinted in Anton Pavlovich Chekhov, *Anton Chekhov's Selected Stories: Texts of the Stories, Comparison of Translations, Life and Letters, Criticism*, sel. and ed. Cathy Popkin (New York: Norton, 2014), 658–64.

Feinberg, Barbara. *Welcome to Lizard Motel: Children, Stories, and the Mystery of Making Things Up* (Boston: Beacon Press, 2004).

Felski, Rita. *Uses of Literature* (Malden, MA: Blackwell, 2008).

Finke, Michael. *Seeing Chekhov: Life and Art* (Ithaca, NY: Cornell University Press, 2005).

Freud, Sigmund. "Dostoevsky and Parricide" (1928). In *Writings on Art and Literature*, foreword by Neil Hertz (Stanford, CA: Stanford University Press, 1997), 234–56.

Gessen, Masha. "Found in Translation." *New York Times*, December 28, 2014.

Greenleaf, Monika. *Pushkin and Romantic Fashion: Fragment, Elegy, Orient, Irony* (Stanford, CA: Stanford University Press, 1994).

Lopate, Phillip. "Chekhov for Children," reprinted in *Against Joie de Vivre: Personal Essays* (New York: Poseidon Press, 1989).

Mikhailovsky, Nikolai K. *Dostoevsky: A Cruel Talent* (1882), translated by Spencer Cadmus (Ann Arbor, MI: Ardis, 1978).

Morson, Gary Saul. "Prosaics in *Anna Karenina*." *Tolstoy Studies Journal* 1 (1988): 1–12.

Morson, Gary Saul. "The Pevearsion of Russian Literature." *Commentary Magazine* 130(1), July/August 2010: 92–8.

Mortimer, Emily. "How 'Lolita' Escaped Obscenity Laws and Cancel Culture." *New York Times Book Review*, March 2, 2021.

Nabokov, Vladimir. *Lectures on Russian Literature* (New York: Harcourt Brace Jovanovich, 1981).

Nabokov, Vladimir. "On Translating *Eugene Onegin*," *New Yorker*, January 8, 1955: 34.

Nilsen, Don L. F. "Doppelgängers and Doubles in Literature: A Study in Tragicomic Incongruity." *Humor* 11(2), 1998: 111–34.

Overton, Bill. *The Novel of Female Adultery: Love and Gender in Contintental European Fiction, 1830–1900* (London: St. Martin's Press, 1996).

Pushkin, Alexander. *Eugene Onegin* (1833), trans. James E. Falen (Oxford: Oxford University Press, 1995).

Rancour-Laferriere, Daniel. *Tolstoy on the Couch: Misogyny, Masochism and the Absent Mother* (New York: New York University Press, 1998).

Shklovsky, Viktor. "Art as Device," translated by Alexandra Berlina. *Poetics Today* 36(3), September 1, 2015: 151–74.

Stepanov, Andrei. "Lev Shestov on Chekhov." In *Anton Chekhov through the Eyes of Russian Thinkers: Vasilii Rozanov, Dmitrii Merezhkovskii and Lev Shestov*, edited by Olga Tabachnikova; translated by Olga Tabachnikova and Adam Ure; trans. ed. Adam Ure (London, Anthem Press, 2010), 169–74.

Taylor, Romy. "Champagne for the Brain: Reading and Writing 'Onegin' Stanzas with American Undergraduates." *Pushkin Review/Пушкинский Вестник* 6(7), 2003: 151–60.

Tepperman, Lorne, Patrizia Albanese, Sasha Stark, and Nadine Zahlan. *The Dostoevsky Effect: Problem Gambling and the Origins of Addiction* (Don Mills, Ontario: Oxford University Press, 2013).

Tolstoy, Leo. *Anna Karenina* (1877), trans. Richard Pevear and Larissa Volokhonsky (New York: Viking 2001).

Tynianov, Yuri. "On Khlebnikov" (1928). Trans. in Ainsley Morse and Philip Redko, *Permanent Evolution: Selected Essays on Literature, Theory and Film* (Brookline, MA: Academic Studies Press, 2019), 217–29.

Tynyanov, Yury. *The Death of the Vazir-Mukhtar* (1927). Trans. Anna Kurkina Rush and Christopher Rush (New York: Columbia University Press, 2021).

Waters, Sasha. "Remixing Chekhov." In *Chekhov for the 21st Century*, ed. Carol Apollonio and Angela Brintlinger (Bloomington, IN: Slavica, 2012), 349–54.

INDEX

Index

Index